D1022086

For the Sake of the Gospel

For the Sake of the Gospel

Edward Schillebeeckx

CROSSROAD • NEW YORK

1990

The Crossroad Publishing Company
370 Lexington Avenue, New York, N.Y. 10017

Translated by John Bowden from the Dutch
Om het behoud van het evangelie,
Evangelie verhalen II, published 1988 by Uitgeverij H. Nelissen, Baarn.

Printed in the United States of America

Library of Congress Cataloging-in-Publication Data

Schillebeeckx, Edward, 1914–
[Om het behoud van het evangelie. English]
For the sake of the gospel / Edward Schillebeeckx ; [translated by John Bowden from the Dutch].
p. cm.
Translation of: Om het behoud van het evangelie.
Includes bibliographical references.
ISBN 0-8245-0989-7
1. Catholic Church—Sermons. 2. Sermons, English—Translations from Dutch. 3. Sermons, Dutch—Translations into English.
I. Title.
BX1756.5.S353054 1990
252'.02—dc20 89-27030
CIP

TO THE READER

Faith, theology and preaching are difficult to separate, certainly for a theologian. But one can discover what a theologian really thinks from her or his preaching. This book offers interim testimony to this.

The prompting for it came from many sides. No sooner had *God Among Us* appeared, in the Netherlands in 1982 and in English in 1983, than there were requests for another collection, especially from the United States, where the book became prescribed reading for catechetics in a number of Religious Departments and Divinity Schools.

But sermons are not articles. One is invited to give them on particular days in the year by a Christian community. They are related to the scriptural reading appointed for the Sunday. On the basis of that, there comes into being, in interaction with the community of faithful present, a text for preaching. This is not the same as a theological contribution where one chooses the text and context oneself. The two genres are organically connected, but they are not the same.

In this book you will find a second series of homilies, along with some meditations and articles which together form a whole.

I have called the book *For the Sake of the Gospel*; it is of course a sequel to *God among Us*, but here and there, certainly in the sermons which have been given over the past two years, there are also glimpses of what will be in the third volume of my christological trilogy, which I hope will be ready in the middle of 1989. So in this interim work, too, I hope to show that proclamation and theology belong closely together – like prayer and politics.

Where there are notes they come at the end of the chapter. There are biblical references and details of where the homilies or addresses were given and/or published at the end of the book.

Nijmegen, 12 October 1988 Edward Schillebeeckx OP

CONTENTS

I · Snatches of Jesus' Message and Lifestyle
The freedom of the children of God

1

May one heal on the sabbath?

(Luke 14.1-7)

At the word of welcome

The two scripture readings (Numbers 15.32-36 and Luke 14.1-7), both of which are about a transgression of the sabbath law, contradict each other quite markedly. Nevertheless this demonstrates in a very telling way how Jesus wanted to see the Torah or law of Moses as the will of God and how he did not.

Homily

In chapter 14 of his Gospel Luke makes use of the 'symposium' as a literary means of providing a meaningful framework within his Gospel narrative for 'logia' or sayings of Jesus which had been handed down in isolation.

Table-talk was a well-known form of literary composition in both the Roman and the Jewish world. But it also happened in real life. Indeed prominent Jews even had the custom of inviting guests to a meal each week after the sabbath synagogue service at the sixth hour. This is the setting which Luke gives to his account of Jesus' third healing on the sabbath. Today's story as a whole is peculiar to the Gospel of Luke; the other three Gospels do not know it. It also displays a very subtle piece of composition by Luke.

Previously Luke has suggested a situation that has been tense from the start, not for Jesus but among all those invited (this is understandable from what the reader already knows from the preceding chapters of the Gospel; in the story the irritation surrounding Jesus reaches a climax). For his part Jesus shows himself to be clearly aware of the tension among his host and fellow-guests. For Luke makes the Pharisees watch Jesus closely, almost spy on him; they want to trap him over the question whether he will observe all the sabbath laws strictly. Suddenly they are all confronted with a sick person: a man with the dropsy, whose arms and legs and whole body have swollen up as a result of too much fluid – often a sign of complete physical deterioration. I once saw someone suffering in this way: it aroused both compassion and distaste in me. The story does not say whether this man was also one of the guests or how he came to be in the company. That does not matter; stories of this kind do not call for clarification. The important thing is that the presence of this sick man brings matters to a head both for the others present and for Jesus. They know Jesus as someone who is concerned about sick people. But it is the sabbath, and on that day one may not work. And this circumstance seems to decide whether one's healing is in the name of God, from good motives, or in the name of Beelzebub, from bad motives.

In a Palestinian law book, from about the same time as the New Testament, we read that one might not give help to a beast that was calving on the sabbath day, even if the calf should fall into a well (CD = Cairo Damascus document 11.13-14). So Jesus was very well aware of the suspicions of the Pharisees and indeed of his prominent host. But he challenges them and poses a question: not whether one can work on the sabbath – for Jesus too thought that that was not allowed – but: 'May one heal on the sabbath, i.e. help a fellow human being in need?' The answer seems clear; no one dares to contradict him, but they do not explicitly support him either. The question compromises those present. The tension comes to a climax when it becomes clear to all who are there that Jesus is indeed going to heal this sick man in their presence.

But Jesus himself heightens the challenge: this time he does not just heal the man with an authoritative word, which even New Testament Pharisees could hardly call 'work on the sabbath'. Jesus heals him through an action, something he does with his hands, in order to show that this action is '*work*', work in the legal sense of the word which is forbidden on the sabbath day of rest. And in order to give all this 'body', he takes a firm hold of the swollen-up sick man. The Greek literally is: taking him firmly in his grasp (*epilambanein*) he healed him and... then let him go again. These are the two images which Luke uses here to make the event vivid. They are images which were also used at the time for wrestlers, grasping each other firmly in order as it were to compress the tensed muscles of the opponent and then suddenly release him again, so as finally to get the better of him. Unfortunately, the translations quite fail to indicate this firm grip by Jesus, which is really the whole point of the story, Luke wants to say that purely from a legal point of view what Jesus did was indeed work on the sabbath day, but work which healed a sick man.

In order to involve the others even more in this clearly strenuous work, Jesus again addresses those present in order to make them so to speak accomplices in what he has done. He now challenges them in an even more personal way: 'Which of you, having a child or an animal that has fallen into a well, will not immediately pull him out on a sabbath day?' They all know that they would do this spontaneously. So they keep silent, compromised by the happening against their will. But Luke makes another subtle addition to the text. Which of you would not pull his *own* son or ox out of a well on the sabbath?... Would they also do this for *someone else's* son or ox? Jesus does not criticize the sabbath law here in any way; he criticizes the deficiency in real human love as a result of which relations have gone wrong and the sabbath does not serve men and women, but men and women serve the sabbath. In Luke 6.5, Luke had already said: 'The Son of man is Lord of the sabbath'; in other words: the sabbath is for human beings and not human beings for the sabbath. God wanted the weekly day of rest to be for wholeness, wellbeing and human relaxation, not to lay a new yoke on people!

That is the short but vigorous message of today's gospel.

2

The urgency of dedication to the cause of Jesus, the Christ

(Luke 10.1-9)

At the word of welcome

Reapers, harvesters who have to bring in the ripe grain, know that when rain and heavy downpours threaten, the harvest can be completely ruined. The critical question is sometimes: will we get the harvest in in time? For in that case it is a question of get it in or go under, and for poor people this can be a matter of life or death.

In the Gospel of Luke, Jesus' sending out of seventy-two disciples to bring the good news of the approach of the kingdom of God is compared with the dedicated haste of reapers and binders who want to get the harvest in before disaster strikes.

Today Luke's church presents some rules of conduct for its missionaries and those whom it sends out, here represented as harvesters, which are to govern their mission.

Homily

The sending out of the Twelve is described in all four Gospels, but the story of Jesus' sending out of seventy-two disciples is a unique feature of the Gospel of Luke: indeed the story may be regarded as Luke's own composition. The reason why Luke talks about two missions emerges from the context of his story: the harvest is so overwhelming that not only the official Twelve but many other Christians are called to bring it in. Moreover, while Luke keeps the special significance of the term 'the Twelve', which for him was already a traditional one, at the same time in the book of Acts he lets the role of the Twelve fade more into the background. This book is less about the apostolic work of the Twelve than about the church work of other Christians. The apostolic fruits of the Spirit are not tied to the appearance of the Twelve. In Jewish eyes, seventy-two is a round number: a very large number.

According to the story Jesus sends out seventy-two disciples in pairs. Think of the church custom which emerges from the New Testament: we read there about Paul and Barnabas, Peter and John, Paul and Silas, Jude and Silas, Barnabas and Mark, and so on. Nowhere does the New Testament talk about a one-man show. (Last Sunday we celebrated 'Peter and Paul'.)

It is said that the disciples who have been sent out must bring in the harvest. In the Old Testament the harvest was the image of the time of the last judgment; however, in Luke the harvest is an image for the worldwide spread of the gospel of the kingdom of God. The disciples are sent out by Jesus in order to say and do, as his representatives, what Jesus did: to proclaim the approaching kingdom of God and make this approaching kingdom visible by healing their fellow men and women and bringing them to themselves: as Luke puts it, healing the sick and proclaiming the kingdom of God. Precisely through this making whole of people who are bruised, hurt and tormented by bad dreams, it is demonstrated to all that the kingdom of God has come very near to men and women. What Jesus himself had done in sending out the Twelve is repeated in the disciples sent out by the church.

That really is the obvious heart of Luke's story and therefore it is taken for granted. What Luke wants to impress more on his hearers and readers, who already know that gospel, is rather the *way in which* the disciples must perform the task of preaching the gospel. In pastoral and psychological terms we would now say that as a community leader Luke (at least here) is concerned with the pastoral *attitude* of those who are sent out, the messengers, and not with the content of the message. And in that case it is striking that here Luke refers back to the rules for the early Christian communities, long known, which the apostolic messengers who were sent out at that time by the ancient churches of Jerusalem and Galilee had to obey; the material of Luke's story comes from the so-called Q tradition, which is older than Mark's story (Mark 6.6b-13). In Matthew and Mark the rules are less radical; there they are adapted to new circumstances in the world and the church. Luke, however, refers to very old rules of conduct for mission. On a first reading we might even find these old rules rough and crude: those who are sent out may not carry any money, nor even a knapsack with iron rations; they may not even wear sandals: moreover they may not greet anyone on the way.

Is there sometimes an expression of mission fanaticism here? I don't think so. Already in the Old Testament 'Do not greet anyone on the way' (e.g. II Kings 4.29; Ps.129.8) was well known as a sign of urgency and of dedication to one cause, to which all else had to yield. In the East, 'greeting' someone is not like the Western 'Hello' or a brief 'How are you?' in passing. In the East, greeting someone on a journey is not just a matter of stopping and standing for a short time, but involves sitting down, starting conversations, debating, arguing; it also involves gaining information and handing on news; at the same time doing bits of business and gossiping about others; passing on rumours, and so on. All this is greeting in the Eastern sense of the term, and that is forbidden to the preacher. Why? It would not occur to me, but for Luke, given the context of this story, the reason seems to be that 'greeting' may not be given to any chance passer-by; greeting must be reserved for greetings to 'houses', i.e. to whole families, and to 'cities', which at that time consisted in a network of families. Luke says explicitly: 'Whatever house you enter, first say: "Peace be to this house!"' – in other words a greeting. The proclaimer greets in elaborate Eastern fashion the *family* which receives him or her. This in fact points to the specific historical way in which primitive Christianity spread, namely through the ancient extended family.

In this story from the Gospel of Luke we really hear something about the missionary strategy of the earliest Christian communities: the miracle that has to be achieved in part involves the organization of time and forces, which are not available without limit. Here we are not listening to a norm for missionary work at all times. But this old strategy is still a pointer even for us. In every situation the preachers must keep looking for the face they are to give to the church community; they must also look for the appropriate way in which the old gospel story can be handed on to coming generations in changed circumstances. Perhaps in our time this is no longer the family; moreover we no longer have the old type of family. The reading from this Gospel of Luke challenges us to look for the new appropriate places where modern preachers of the kingdom of God must begin and get started. Where are they to give 'elaborate Eastern greetings': in a great monastery like the Albertinum? In a Père Chenu fellowship? In a Tolsteegsingel? In a Dominican parish? In some critical community? In the 8 May movement? Or somewhere in a suburb in Dukenburg or de Goorn and de Hoorn?[1] Or wherever one encounters fellow human being as Christians, men or women? In other words, where do our greetings begin? And where do we not give greetings?

Today's gospel will certainly pose a dilemma to all of us: on the one hand we are cut off from particular pastoral possibilities which we fancy : 'Greet no one on the way' (Luke 10.4b), and on the other hand other pastoral ways are opened up: 'Whatever house you enter, first say: "Peace be to this house!"' (Luke 10.5). – It seems to be a matter of to greet or not to greet, and to do so at the appropriate moment. That would mean that you refuse to carry on superficial conversations in order to make deep conversations possible. It would mean that you devote all your strength and time to long, tranquil, authentic and therefore comforting meetings. In this way what is meant symbolically in the greeting, in the best case, must become reality: grace, abiding happiness. It would mean that we weave a net of like-minded contacts within which we also receive 'the others'. It would mean that we are never just on the way, driven on by all possible purposes, but that where people encounter one another we are always at our destination. There is still life to arouse; there are still wonders to tell... and time is pressing.

That is how this Gospel of Luke formulates the problem of all pastoral work, i.e. of the way in which Christians deal with fellow human beings at the level of proclamation. And the story ends with the words: 'The seventy-two returned with joy, saying, "Lord, even the demons are subject to us in your name!"' (Luke 10.17). Not even the Twelve always managed that, says the Gospel of Luke barely ten verses earlier (9.40)!

It is striking that in this Gospel of Luke there is no mention of *where* the seventy-two had gone and *from where* they returned after their mission. All that is said is that they were sent out *by Jesus* and that they returned *to Jesus*. Preachers do not set out as adventurers: in their mission they remain 'followers of Jesus'.

So a last lesson that this Gospel of Luke seeks to give to all preachers of the kingdom of God – for us this means men and women, here and now – is this: they are sent as lambs among wolves; in other words, preachers of the kingdom of God are defenceless, as defenceless as Jesus himself and the kingdom of God that he proclaims and brings closer. Preachers have only the support of defenceless but strong love. Amen.

Note

1. The Dominican houses mentioned are experimental centres alongside classical parishes.

3

'Ephphatha', which means 'Be opened'

(Mark 7.31-37)

At the word of welcome

There is a striking paradox in the official compilation of the liturgy for today. In the first reading from Isaiah 35.4-7a we hear of God's punitive judgment on pagan peoples, while at the same time there is a prophecy of the desert blooming only in and for Israel (Isa.35.1-2,7) and God coming near to save in Israel for the benefit of the sick and the crippled in Israel (Isa.35.5-6). But in its vision of the messianic Jesus the Gospel of Mark turns this story almost radically upside down.

Homily

Here Mark tells of the healing by Jesus of someone who is deaf and dumb. In order to describe the situation precisely he uses a specific Greek word (*mogilalos*); in his story this does not so much denote someone who cannot speak at all, a dumb man, but someone with a speech impediment, who articulates badly because of deafness. The impediment in his speech is really a symptom of his real illness: genuine deafness, a situation of not being able to hear anything and therefore not being able to understand. There are two dimensions in this story of Mark's. And on both levels the fact of not hearing and not understanding plays a significant and critical role.

So we must first listen to what this physical healing of a deaf person has to say to us, and then we must go on to listen to this story within the plot or the intrigue in the broader context of the Gospel of Mark. For here the physical miracle takes on a fundamentally new significance.

I. The healing of a deaf-mute

'He was already going round doing good.' Mark describes the healing by Jesus in accordance with the model of healing practices that we know from Hellenistic Judaism and Hellenistic Jewish Christianity. We know similar incidents from the historical books of the Roman writers Pliny, Tacitus and Suetonius. Mark's story is very true to life, at least for this time. The model is classical, as it were well-tried. It has about five elements which constantly recur. The sick person is taken aside; originally the purpose of this was to keep the methods and practices of healing used by the miracle workers of the time secret from the bystanders. The miracle-worker touches the sick part: the diseased tooth, the sick ear, the dumb tongue, and so on. In antiquity, moreover, healing power was attributed to spittle: in his *Natural History* Pliny tells a whole story about it (*Historia Naturae* 28, 4, 7); spittle also had a prophylactic power, like an amulet, especially against the demon of sickness. Therefore the use of spittle was later incorporated into the rite of baptism. In Hellenistic stories, for the miracle-worker to look up to heaven and sigh or draw a deep breath is also part of a miraculous event; it indicates that the miracle worker is not doing this miracle in his own strength but drawing on supernatural powers for it. He has to allow the alien power as it were to come over him. Moreover miracle workers make use of an incomprehensible strange word, a kind of spell, a hocus-pocus. As to the genre, the word *ephphatha*, which is difficult to place, formally performs the same function in this story. So the style of the story in Mark is that of a classic miracle story as this was known all over the Hellenistic Jewish and pagan world of the time. Jesus heals a handicapped person; he is always concerned for handicapped, sick and poor people. His concern goes out to them.

However, Mark robs the word *ephphatha*, which was a somewhat strange one even for Jews, of its magic power because he gives an explanatory translation of it and this contains a radical demystification of the incomprehensible word. Mark explicitly says that 'ephphatha' means 'be opened'. Moreover Jesus is not really addressing the sick organ, as did miracle workers of his time, but the sick man. He personalizes or personifies the event. There is a personal relationship between Jesus and the sick man, and that alone already distinguishes this miracle from what a Hellenistic miracle worker did. The reaction of the amazed bystanders clearly indicates what is involved; they said, 'He has done all things good and beautifully (*kalos*)'. The translations to some degree disguise the fact that here Mark is quoting literally the last verse of the creation story according to the Greek version of the book of Genesis (Gen.1.31 according to the Greek Septuagint translation), and moreover in the next half-verse in fact refers to Isaiah 35.4-6: 'Then the eyes of the blind shall be opened, and the ears of the deaf unstopped; then shall the lame man leap like a hart, and the tongue of the dumb sing for joy.' Here messianic salvation, eschatological redemption, is celebrated.

The praise of the bystanders interprets Jesus' action as messianic action; through Jesus' action the damaged and wounded creation is restored: 'And God saw that it was good.' Now God sees that what Jesus does is good. The miracle of Jesus is already somewhat different from accounts of what Hellenistic miracle workers did: for anyone who believes in Jesus the Christ, the dawning of the new creation is realized in his actions. With Jesus the new creation is coming into effect, the messianic time is dawning. This is a first message of a messianic healing story which cannot be eliminated. But in the closer and above all the wider context of the Gospel story, this story of a typical messianic wonder takes on deeper significance. And this is what Mark is concerned to convey to us.

II. Anyone who does not listen to the gospel is deaf and dumb

For a start, Mark sets the event which he relates in the pagan areas around Galilee. In a dispute, immediately preceding this story, in pagan Syro-Phoenicia about what is pure for Jews and therefore what is pagan or unclean (Mark 7.14-23), it becomes clear that Jesus also opens Jewish table-fellowship to pagans; Jews may also eat pagan food. But the disciples do not understand that: from a Jewish point of view this is nonsense – it cannot be! After that Mark makes Jesus travel in a bizarre zig-zag route from pagan Tyre via a pagan detour, round Jewish Galilee, to the heart of the pagan Decapolis. It is here that the healing of the deaf and dumb man takes place (although it is not said that he is a pagan).

To have some idea of what this somewhat crazy route means, we have to shift it to a map of England or the United States. Jesus wants to travel, say, from Bristol to London, but he avoids the whole of the Thames Valley, which in this setting represents Jewish 'Galilee', and goes from Bristol to London via Northampton and Cambridge. Or he wants to travel from New York to Washington but avoids Philadelphia and Baltimore and travels via Buffalo and Pittsburgh. A truly crazy journey! It is not that Mark was unfamiliar with the geographical setting of these cities: he had his own purpose in describing this journey. Here, in Mark's view, the openness of the Jewish gospel of Jesus to the pagan world was already proclaimed by Jesus himself, and not just by Paul or by Peter under pressure from Paul. Thus without denying the miracle of a physical healing or forcing it into the background, the Gospel of Mark, by inserting this tradition of a healing done by Jesus into the wider context of the Gospel, almost imperceptibly passes over to a deeper symbolic level. In the wider context of his Gospel Mark indicates the inability of the disciples and people generally to understand Jesus' person and mission. Already before (Mark 7.18) and also after (Mark 8.17-21) the healing of the deaf and dumb man the disciples are criticized for this inability. This takes up the complaints of the prophets who criticize the people for its blind eyes, deaf ears and hardened heart. Some verses before this miracle story Mark makes Jesus say: 'Hear me *and understand*' (Mark 7.14). But the disciples do not understand; only a pagan woman who does believe Jesus' word, a Syro-Phoenician woman, is not deaf and dumb (7.24-30). She has listened to what Jesus says, considered it, and accepted it: she believes his words.

And then Mark weaves the tradition of the healing of a deaf mute into his story of the understanding or lack of understanding of Jesus' gospel (7.31-37). He wants his hearers, readers, Jews and Gentiles, to note that only Jesus can open their ears to the gospel. In the last resort, through and thanks to the story of a miraculous healing, it is a matter of opening our ears to the gospel of Jesus the Christ. Belief in the gospel is a gift of Jesus. Without grace any man or woman remains as it were deaf and dumb in respect of the Good News (see Mark 4.11-12). The physical benefit of the healing of a deaf mute becomes a real symbol of the miracle of faith and the understanding of faith.

PS A note for the present-day reader of Mark

To conclude: it is a distinctive feature of the Gospel of Mark that Jesus commands those who have benefited from his good actions to be silent. It is also a distinctive feature of Mark that the more firmly this command to be silent is impressed on people, the more rapidly and enthusiastically they begin to proclaim the action. This seems to me to be a literary means used by the evangelist Mark to make clear to his readers that the miracle which Jesus does quietly, and not in a sensational way, of its own power begins to speak loudly as a revelation of God through the mouth of the one who can see the miracle. Finally, the miracle is taken up into the kerygma and in this way becomes a new source of power: in the proclamation it takes on a new function through the power of the witness of faith given by Jesus' disciples. The miracle is handed on as something which has changed and renewed the life of men and women: the bystanders are also witnesses to this. Not just the healing of the sick but also the renewal of life which this brings about in many who follow Jesus, see the miracle and in this way come to believe, are taken up in the retelling of a traditional story of a healing miracle performed by Jesus.

And precisely this renewal of life is the greatest miracle within the gospel story of Mark! For the proclamation of the witnesses is followed by the final reaction of the crowd: 'He has done all things well; he even makes the deaf hear and the dumb speak' (Mark 7.37).

That is the reaction of the people to the proclamation of those who were told to keep silent, but who cannot but bear witness to what they saw and what had changed their life for good. Speaking in proclamation, the story itself, also has a productive significance which brings about human liberation. In the Middle Ages many exegetes like Bede and Thomas Aquinas stressed the deeper significance of the story of the deaf mute above all and almost one-sidedly. They said: 'Those are deaf and dumb who do not go on to tell what they confess as faith.'

So the question to us is whether or not in this sense we ourselves are the deaf mute, the real subject of this story of Mark's!

4

The unworthy servant

(Luke 17.5-10)

At the word of welcome

The organizers of today's liturgy have connected Luke's story of the unworthy servant with the famous Habakkuk text (1.2-3) on which Paul founded his doctrine of 'justification by faith'. But perhaps the Gospel of Luke, which also has in mind rich, or at least well-to-do, Christians, is concerned with very pastoral questions, of vital importance if things are to go well in a church community of faith.

Homily

As in various readings on previous Sundays, so in chapter 17 Luke combines words and sayings of Jesus into a literary whole and does so in a very distinctive way, for the second half of the pericope which has been read out, about the unworthy servant, is again peculiar to the Gospel of Luke: it cannot be found anywhere in the other Gospels. At a first reading this story disturbs, indeed shocks us. Usually in his parables and sayings Jesus turns upside down the social rules which apply in our day-to-day life: things always happen quite differently in the kingdom of God from the way in which they do in human society. In the kingdom of God a parasite, a worker who begins at the eleventh hour, gets just as much as someone who has worked all day, enduring the heat of the sun. Moreover, there are no master-servant relationships in the kingdom of God.

Today in the same Gospel of Luke we suddenly hear that Jesus seems to compare God, the Lord, with a worldly ruler who commands his servant, a slave who comes back in the evening dead tired from much work in the field, first to prepare a meal for his master; only when the master has eaten his fill may the over-weary servant eat the rest. For all this drudgery the servant is then not even thanked by his master: he is forced into the social role of the poor, unworthy servant, who has done his duty and what he has been commanded. That is what being a servant is; that is what he has been hired for. This situation is then compared with work for the kingdom of God. A perplexing gospel! Are there then still master-servant relationships?

But are we reading this story properly? Elsewhere in the New Testament God is compared with a master who comes home in the evening from a good dinner and meets some servants who are still awake. Glad to find faithful servants, the master himself begins to prepare a meal for them and he serves them at table himself. This is indeed how we hear Jesus talking about God. That is what God is like; that is what Jesus is like. But what about this, the unworthy servant in the same Gospel of Luke? This picture of God does not fit Luke's Gospel.

Something quite different must be meant. And indeed this is not a parable in which God's doings are compared with the behaviour of a lord in a hierarchically ordered society, who does not think servants worth even a word of thanks. That is what goes on in the world. But Luke is not comparing *God* with this patriarchal Lord; he is comparing God and the one who has been sent, Jesus, and his disciples, with the servant, not with the master. If that is the case, the text suddenly takes on all kinds of new perspectives for us which we had not noticed at a first reading.

In that case it becomes clear that the first two short verses which come from another tradition that is also common to Mark and Matthew are very deliberately connected by Luke with his own tradition of the unworthy servant. It had already struck me that in recent years more exegetes have pointed to the possibility that the Gospel of Luke is addressed to a Christian community of well-to-do middle-class Christians, to relatively rich Christians. Many signs in the Gospel and in Acts point in this direction; at least that certain rich Christians are making too much of a mark on the community. Socially well-to-do Christians are often tempted to boast about their achievements in church work, and also about their status and place, with the danger of excessive self-esteem, to the detriment and disgust of the so-called lesser ones, the little ones in the community of faith as the church of Christ. The institution of, or rather the emphasis on, the presbyters in Luke's community is also connected historically with limiting the great influence of rich Christians in the house communities, who often had excessive influence in the community of faith.

The pericope begins with a request by the disciples which Luke has in common with the other Gospels: 'Increase our faith.' The lack of faith which is mentioned in the other Gospels and because of which the request is made for an increase in faith takes on quite a different significance in Luke. These rich Christians in the Gospel of Luke are not of little faith – they want a megalomanic faith, i.e. one which overrates itself, that does miracles and achieves great successes.

They want a kind of sensational faith, one which the whole community of faith will stare at. Jesus disillusions them: if only you had as much faith as a mustard seed! Of course this is not the faith of a mustard seed, which does not have any faith at all; here the degree of their faith is compared with the tiny size of a mustard seed. We know from other parables that the mustard seed was regarded as a particularly tiny seed. So if one had only a tiny little bit of real faith, only a grain of faith, then with a word one could transplant a mulberry tree into the middle of the sea: one would only have to say, 'Be uprooted and plant yourself in the sea'! Mulberry trees were known, as they still are, to have particularly firm roots! In contrast to bushes, the roots of which largely grow horizontally and almost above ground, the roots of mulberry trees, like those of oaks, go deep into the ground and withstand the strongest storms. But they will not withstand the smallest grain of authentic faith in God. Of course Jesus is exaggerating, deliberately; we say in a learned way that he is exaggerating in order to attack and disillusion the striving of particular Christians for a sensational faith. Even a small amount of faith can do a great deal.

Here Jesus is rejecting the tendency to subjective certainty in faith: the prayer 'Increase our faith' is as old as the relationship between human beings and God. The disciples want to see great successes as a result of their faith. But according to Jesus you must take the little faith that you have more seriously and not seek to escape because your faith is still so small. Exaggeration and disillusionment here lie very close together. This is clearly aimed against excessive claims about oneself. And it is precisely here that the saying about the unworthy servant fits in very well. Jesus is warning his disciples against the error of overestimating oneself: feeling oneself to be important in the church, the irreplacable man or woman in the whole show. Here Jesus is attacking excessive boasting and loud talk about achievements in work for people and the church.

Jesus is not presented here as this lord who commands servants in a patriarchal way. This unworthy servant is Jesus himself, who does all that the Father has commanded him; the apostles must also be unworthy servants like Jesus, who do all that Jesus has told them. We too often say in everyday life, after someone has thanked us for one service or another: 'Not at all', 'Don't mention it', or 'The thanks are all mine'. In Spain and Flanders they use a remarkable expression for this, 'De nada', 'It's nothing'; what I did was nothing; and indeed usually it is nothing. But the servant in the story had worked himself to the bone all day and even then says, 'It's nothing'. That is precisely what Luke wants to convey here: 'Not at all, don't thank me.' Such people do not feel this as a necessity; it is a matter of doing an obvious service for someone who to whom one has a duty: disinterested service without extra aims or extra reward; being glad to have been able to do something for someone else who, by being given your attention, becomes someone who you love. That is how things are in the kingdom of God, and our human world must be a model of this, give a foretaste of it.

Exert yourself, give all, do other things after the work you have to do, like the unworthy servant who on top of everything else has to make dinner and after that could say cheerfully, 'Not at all, master – at your service, master', and mean it. The message of today's gospel is as simple as that.

5

The merciless servant

(Matthew 18.21-35)

At the word of welcome

Every seventh year there was a year of jubilee in which all debts were remitted, so that Israel should be a land of righteousness and love.

In the New Testament we are asked to remit debts and offer forgiveness to seventy times seven.

Let us pray in silence for power to forgive others their debts to us.

Homily

The story of the merciless servant seems simple, but this parable has very deep roots. A king wants to make a reckoning with his servants. Someone appears before him who owes an incredibly large sum of money: 10,000 talents, around 15 million dollars. The first audience for this parable might perhaps have thought of a satrap or governor, someone who had not yet handed over the fiscal contribution of his province. But even in that case the size of the sum surpasses all imaginable reality. The debtor cannot, of course, pay such a sum of money. The parable is evidently a preparation for something else. First the king makes use of his right as a ruler: he orders that the debtor shall be sold, along with his family and household. However, the servant asks for the deadline to be shifted and then promises, probably in anxiety and in distress, that he will pay back everything. Hearing this, the master has pity and generously forgives him the whole debt.

Hardly has this man gone out than he meets a colleague, a fellow servant who owes him 100 denarii – say about 50 dollars. But as the Greek text puts it, the servant insists on his rights: a debt is a debt; you owe me 50 dollars. Even worse, when this other servant, in almost the same words as he himself had used, asks for more time to pay, the first servant takes him to law: he has him thrown into prison until the debtor has paid off everything through his own work or until relatives ransom him. Later on the king hears of this, summons the servant to him and says, 'Should you not have done to him what I did to you?' As a result the first servant is now treated in just the same way, since he is condemning himself through his own behaviour. Now the law which he revered and imposed on a third party is going to be applied to him, too; he must pay off his great debt as soon as possible.

That is the story. But what does this parable really mean?

In many parables, even in today's parable, Jesus, who tells the parables, reverses human legal relationships. By his proclamation and praxis of the kingdom of God Jesus relativizes for his fellow men and women the often hard-fought-for principle of 'insisting on one's rights' (even, indeed above all, when one is right). The one who works from the last hour gets just as much as those who work from the first hour. For Jesus, the praxis of the kingdom of God seems to be alternative action, in contrast to what people are usually inclined to do in our society. Jesus does not defend people who do evil, but he does go and stand beside them. He unmasks the intentions of those who are zealous for God and justice when they do not act for the salvation and well-being of others, but to the detriment of human beings, men and women. Insisting on rights can in fact include the excommunication of people who have already been outcast, in whose case there is whispering behind their backs: '...divorced, homosexual, heretic, married priest!'

The coming kingdom of God knows nothing of the very human but often hypocritical logic of strict justice. Jesus wants to give hope to people who from a social and human point of view, according to the rules of our society, no longer have any hope. People who insist on their rights defend 'unassailable laws' but in so doing injure particular vulnerable human beings who are socially already wounded. Jesus opposes this human, legalistic justice in which these human laws result in the grim exclusion of the other party. For Jesus, the principle of human justice – a debt is a debt – is never the last word. Jesus takes the part of those without an advocate, those with a great many accusers who cast out their fellow men and women with an appeal to law and justice, pointing with their finger, and thus giving them one more kick, in the then sanctimonious feeling that they themselves are not 'like that sinner there' – as the parable of the Pharisee and the publican indicates in a razor-sharp portrait!

The technique of this parable of the merciless servant, which is what actually makes the parable work, is based on the discord, the inconsistency, between two comparable scenes, in which in almost the same words two debtors ask for more time to pay. The first is forgiven his great debt, but when it comes to a third party he himself insists on what applies in the normal course of justice: debts, great or small, must be paid. Because both scenes in this story are interconnected, it becomes clear to the listeners that they must distance themselves from the servant's behaviour, although he was literally insisting on his rights; the third party indeed owed him 50 dollars. The parable illustrates how out of keeping with the gospel is the behaviour of the one who stubbornly insists in all circumstances on his own rights when God himself is so gracious to him. The one who had experienced an almost inconceivable act of mercy does not seem ready to forgive a third party what by comparison is a ridiculously small debt. While this merciless servant 'insisted on his rights', he did not realize that in such circumstances right and law lose their authority and power, because they do not serve human beings, but wound them, trap them in the mire. Even the most holy sabbath is for human beings, and not vice versa.

The parable seeks to set off in the listener a process, a new understanding of the relationship among men and women, which furthers the reality of the kingdom of God. The excessively large sum that is owed, out of all proportion, is not just or even above all a narrative trick to bring out effectively how out of keeping is the behaviour of the servant who is forgiven, far less in this context is it an expression of the boundless guilt of men and women over against God, as many exegetes would explain it. For in this allegorical exegesis we introduce a distinction which is not intended by the text, between guilt towards God and guilt towards our fellow human beings. And it is in no sense the intention of biblical parables to oppress men and women under their guilt towards God. In the story the enormous sum serves primarily to bring out the unimaginable degree of God's mercy, just as on the other side the laughably small debt of the second servant is meant to show clearly how obviously the listener might expect mercy of this first servant after his generous remission. But the merciless servant acts against all the expectations aroused by the parable. That is the point of the whole story.

The characteristic and unexpected distinctive Christian nature of this story is that Matthew develops an independent parable of forgiveness which had been handed down to him into a parable of the coming of the kingdom of God. For Matthew it is about the merciful eschatological action of God in the end-time, about his gracious mercy *and* judgment, just as these words are now already addressed to us all and realized in us in Jesus' proclamation and praxis of the kingdom of God. The nucleus of the story is the eschatological quality of the action of God in Jesus. With this parable Jesus is trying to bring his audience really to distance themselves from behaviour towards fellow human beings which is concerned for their own rights, i.e. behaviour which is of this world and not of the kingdom of God. The parable seeks to lure the listeners out of their stronghold of behaviour or modes of action which are built merely on rights. It is not *one's own* rights, but the salvation and welfare of *others* that is the praxis of the kingdom of God – the realization of Jesus' proclamation of the kingdom of God. The experience of the goodness of God makes our goodness to one another not only possible, but also a radical duty, an obligation of the kingdom of God. That is the way in which a Christian must act. Where God has addressed himself so radically to men and women, they in turn can and must also address themselves to their fellow human beings: in forgiveness, reconciliation and the forgiving of debts. From a Christian perspective there is no other principle of action for men and women than the salvation and welfare of fellow human beings, and this includes abandoning one's own rights and, depending on circumstances, also forgiving other people's real debts.

Collectively speaking, among other things this could mean that in the year 2000 the kingdom of God will indeed have come closer to us, or at least could have come closer to us, if Christians from the First World, above all in countries with a predominantly Christian population, could prompt their own states prophetically and make it clear that the forgiveness of the monetary debt of the Third World countries can be a Christian duty for people of the First World.

For us personally, as individual Christians, on a smaller scale, the forgiveness of debt in contrast to a grim insistence on one's own rights can be an urgent task to be repeated daily and – as we should be aware – also among ourselves. If not, then our solemn Sunday praying or singing of the 'Our Father' in the Albertinum, 'Forgive us our debts as we forgive others their debts', will become an eschatological judgment on us – which is finally also the fate of the merciless servant in the parable. After his gracious experience of the remission of his own enormous debt from above he nevertheless demands from a junior fellow-servant a tiny, paltry sum as a matter of life or death. He could have and should have known better.

That is the gospel message that the Gospel of Matthew brings to us today.

6

A conversation with Nicodemus by night

(John 3.1-13)

At the word of welcome

Today we are celebrating the feast and the risk of a solemn religious profession, in which a young man promises to enter our Dominican family for good, to bear witness to the truth as the liberation of men and women. As the gospel story to proclaim for the celebration of the eucharist at this profession he himself suggested to me the conversation between Jesus and Nicodemus by night. His own profession must as it were disappear behind this story of a somewhat timid but authentic searcher after God, Nicodemus, in whom there was no guile.

Homily

The story from the Gospel of John which has just been read out is about a secret, nocturnal conversation between two great religious figures: on the one hand a notable 'teacher of Israel' named Nicodemus, and on the other Jesus whom this Nicodemus calls a 'teacher from God', but who is already identified by the Gospel of John as the 'Son of man', as it were the model man from and of a better world on earth. Nicodemus shuns the clear light of day for this conversation, which is decisive for him. He feels attracted by Jesus, in whom he recognizes the best of the Torah or the Jewish way of life. But he senses something more in Jesus: he is not quite sure what. He wants security; he wants to make a definitive decision. But this can still turn out to be a negative one; therefore he goes to Jesus by night for fear of his colleagues, who have already declared themselves to be against Jesus because he is a threat to their privileged position. But there is also a deeply human motive behind this nocturnal visit, certainly in the Gospel of John, which has a predilection for strong contrasts: darkness and light, shining heavenly spheres and the dark sublunary, day and night, belief and unbelief. Precisely because the heart of the conversation between these two teachers is the theme of belief and unbelief, the still-wavering Nicodemus chooses the half-darkness, the twilight of the late evening. At that time people talk confidentially with one another, above all about questions of faith which affect their own identity. In such conversations one must lay bare one's innermost being. Above all among Eastern people in an agricultural land the darkness removes the inhibitions which can easily be present when people talk about their most intimate being. Then a disarming, open conversation is easier; then people dare to make themselves vulnerable, while expecting the same open vulnerability from their partners in discussion.

Both conversation-partners believe in God, and yet the conversation is about the distinction between belief and unbelief. Nicodemus is a member of the Jewish hierarchy of the scribes or wise men; Jesus, from an official point of view, is a marginal figure from the grass roots, whom Nicodemus nevertheless calls a 'teacher from God', not from a religious institution in opposition to Nicodemus. Nicodemus, a Jew in whom there was no guile, had sought out Jesus to discuss all this. At such a nocturnal conversation both conversation partners must lay bare their innermost thoughts and feelings; and indeed this is what they want to do; both feel compelled to make personal and definitive disclosures of themselves. Jesus lays himself completely open; he says frankly who he is: he comes from God to men and women to show them a good way of life. The remarkable thing about the whole story is that no more is said about Nicodemus, who had taken the initiative in the conversation; he imperceptibly disappears from the story. We do not know, at least from this story, whether Nicodemus overcame his doubts and whether he made his choice for or against Jesus. The Gospel of John leaves the outcome to the grace of God, for people need a new birth from God if they are to be able to recognize Jesus as their own way of life also.

Elsewhere in the Gospel of John Jesus asks seriously, 'Will you too go away?', whereupon the disciples equally seriously ask in reply, 'Lord, to whom else should we go?' What better can the world with its own images and ideologies give us instead? *Either* you let yourself fall into the emptiness and darkness of your finite existence *or* you believe in a mystery which cannot be expressed in words, which embraces you and never lets you go: God, as Jesus showed him in human contours. The abyss of our incomprehensible and often barren world is no deeper nor more real than the abyss of God's mystery, that shows in Jesus the form of love and humanity, of mercy and promise. This rooting of one's own finitude and limitations in the ground of our existence, the mystery of God, discloses itself in human consciousness as a peace beyond words: the incomprehensible certainty of the one who believes. The hidden and often incomprehensible God and the God who reveals himself as a God who 'loves humankind' is one and the same; only the one who believes in God and has this inner peace can also emanate peace and share it with others.

Has this story about Nicodemus anything to do with a religious profession? Not directly. But indirectly, everything! From the outside, 'to make a profession' means to give oneself away – in and through a religious vow – to God and one's fellow human beings in the presence of a Christian community which acts as public witness of the event. But from a deeper perspective, those who make this religious profession are, precisely by this promise, asking that others, God and their brethren, should have mercy on them, that they all, together with God, should affirm, 'Yes, you have a right to be there'; you have a right to be there, in and among us, with all that you have and hold, and with all that you do not have. That is religious profession: it is once again in a special way to be 'justified' in the eyes of God in all your human frailty. Can God not make children of Abraham out of stones, i.e. believers who will move mountains?

No one becomes a Dominican in order to do great things. The question is only: may we, however we are modelled and fashioned, feel at home with everyone as 'people of God' who want to mean and can mean something for our fellow human beings?

Anyone who believes that, Jesus himself said, will do greater things than Jesus himself did. That is quite something! The mystery of such a religious life is reflected in this story of Nicodemus: 'to be a witness of heavenly things'. Before today you chose this gospel because it is such a good expression of yourself and also of the Dominican saying *contemplata aliis tradere*; or, as the gospel puts it, 'We speak of what we have seen'. God is love. To be allowed to be a witness of love in and through one's own human goodness, liberated from oneself to be free for others, is the religious consequence of that and also the heart of the promises made at profession.

Religious life should be a *pointer to God* in the sense that people must be able to say: if this man or woman is already so good, think how good God must be! In the presence of such a person you yourself also feel that you too have a right to be there and that you are not obliterated by the behaviour or the treatment of the other. 'Living from God' for fellow men and women, in all their ups and downs, is not so easy in our time. We too can often no longer speak openly and spontaneously about God as we did in the past: spontaneously, because – grasped and personally moved as we were – we could not 'not speak' about God. But it is towards that *speaking to* and *about* God that the Dominican life is directed: towards training people who can speak in this way, however tentatively. The Dominican life remains a journey of reconnaissance to the heart of life; not by yourself, but with everyone else. Today this journey may perhaps be tentative and searching, but it is nevertheless honest and authentic. In the ancient church they asked the candidate monk, '*Si vere quaeris Deum*', if you are authentically in search of God: then you may become a monk.

That you have chosen this story about Nicodemus for this liturgy says a good deal about yourself. So I need not add any personal comments in public. I congratulate you on your religious profession. In this time of crisis for both the religious life and the priesthood, to have the courage of faith to become a religious is an open sign of hope and certainty to others in the world, a sign of belief that things can and must be different and that there is no reason for pessimism. I hope that may also be the joyful gospel comfort today for your mother, who is here and who taught you the first Christian principles, as also for your family and friends.

7

In memory of her

(Luke 7.36-50)

At the word of welcome

Today's two readings speak of the God who 'loves humankind' but they do so in respect of God's treatment of men and women as sinners. I shall be working the Galatians reading into the prayers. God is not just greater than our human heart and our love; he is also greater than our sinfulness.

Homily

Luke's hope-giving story about a woman who anoints Jesus relates to us today a moving event: on the one hand the forgiveness of a gracious God who 'loves humankind', and on the other hand the disarming conversion of a woman whom Luke calls 'a public sinner', someone who had fallen under the spell of Jesus, the man who was known as one took the side of those at whom people pointed the finger, who had been cast out from the circle of their fellow human beings.

This story from the Gospel of Luke in fact gives one of the key points of what, in the steps of Jesus, 'being a Christian' needs to be. But there is also a hidden side to it, and that is less pleasant. I want to mention it first.

There is a whole prehistory to the story of the woman with the ointment. Originally the woman with the ointment was anything but a public sinner; she had long been a woman apostle of Jesus, just like what Luke then calls 'the Twelve', who are all men. We find the story of the woman with the ointment in all four Gospels. A comparison between these four Gospels reveals a good deal about the original friendliness towards women both of Jesus and of the earliest of all New Testament tradition and about how in the second generation of Christians this friendliness towards women was changed into an antipathy towards them, into an adaptation to the Graeco-Roman structures of a male world. What is common to the four stories is that a woman anoints Jesus; this anointing provokes opposition among the bystanders, but Jesus himself rejects this male opposition and takes sides with the woman. All four Gospels say that. But in Matthew and Luke the woman who was originally, namely in the Galilean tradition which we find in Mark and in the Jerusalem or Bethany tradition which we find in the Gospel of John, a woman apostle of Jesus, becomes a public sinner. Quite a difference, I would think. Jesus had stood for the equal worth of men and women in the Christian community: there are no slaves nor free, no men nor women; in the Christian community all are equal, even in the apostolate, the foundation of the church. Moreover in the earliest traditions we see that there were also women at the head of house communities. But after a time the early church adapted itself to the patriarchal structures of the Graeco-Roman world, in which (officially at least) the woman was forbidden entry to leading positions and offices, whether civil or religious. More recent studies have convincingly analysed the change of climate towards women in the early church, and also in the later parts of the New Testament. In Mark and John Jesus' own defence of the woman is still expressed strongly. We also know from later apocryphal Gospels that there was an enormous dispute in the early church between tendencies friendly towards women and those which were hostile to them.

In Mark and John the woman with the ointment has all the features of the true apostle who follows Jesus, and indeed, in contrast to her male colleagues, follows him even 'under the cross', while the men, even Peter who meanwhile had denied Jesus, had fled. To take the cross upon oneself to the end, to Golgotha, is for Mark and John the very definition of the true apostle, and that is what the women were, while the men left him in the lurch. Moreover in these two Gospels it is also a woman, Mary of Bethany (the one who anoints Jesus), to whom the risen Jesus first appears. That, too, was later removed by men from the New Testament, or at least played down.

During the dispute for or against women our story also shifted. The Gospel of Luke is no longer about a faithful woman apostle who through an anointing has confessed prophetically that Jesus is not just Messiah but a suffering, downtrodden Anointed. It is precisely this which Peter, the male apostle, cannot accept. The woman who at that time was marginalized, and whom Jesus had restored to honour, could accept it: Jesus, the outcast, is the true Messiah. This liberating humanity of Jesus was what had freed this woman. And Luke himself must have known something of the original liberated position of women in the church, for he immediately succeeds his story of the 'penitent sinner' with the names of a number of women who followed Jesus and were his disciples in the full sense of the word.

After the story of the woman with the ointment in the Gospel of Mark, Jesus said: 'Truly, truly (this means: now listen very carefully), I say to you, wherever the gospel is preached in the whole world, what she has done will be told in memory of her' (Mark 14.9). One cannot be proclaiming the gospel if one keeps quiet about this prophetic action of a woman who was the first to confess the suffering Messiah and therefore also could be the first witness of Jesus' resurrection. The woman belongs to the heart of the gospel of Jesus the Christ even more than the male apostles.

We would falsify today's gospel from Luke if we believers did not pay attention to this fact, namely how the story of a faithful woman apostle was gradually changed into a message about a public sinner (sublime though that may be in itself). I had to settle that first; now I shall go briefly into the Christian message which the story of Luke itself offers.

Here Jesus is reproached by the Pharisees for daring to have dealings with an anonymous woman who at the time was known there in Bethany as a prostitute, since that is what is suggested in the passage. Hence the end of the story subtly plays on the word 'love': much is forgiven her because she has loved much, but now in the authentic religious and human sense of love. Simon, the Pharisee, does not make an open comment to Jesus but simply thinks: 'How can it be that the prophet will have anything to do with an outcast woman?' That is how any man in the street thought; that was the common view in society. But Jesus says to him: 'My dear Simon, you are a wise Pharisee, but may I tell you a story?' Pharisees are fond of stories. The pious Pharisee – for that is what Simon was – thereupon says precisely what Jesus expected of him.

But what Jesus is really concerned with is this: listen to what your rabbis tell you (in modern terms, because they have the right doctrine, orthodoxy) but do not follow them in what they do. That also occurs elsewhere in the Gospels. The host does not have Jesus' feet washed by his servants, as was the custom, but a woman who was public sinner did it of her own accord, because she saw something special in Jesus. Correct doctrine, but not the praxis of the kingdom of God: that is the gist of Jesus' criticism. (In parenthesis, here we could also make some criticism of Luke; he too has the correct doctrine, but by changing a story which was originally about a liberated woman in the community of God into a story about a public sinner, he is not doing quite the right thing. Perhaps the story had already been changed in this direction before him, since otherwise Luke shows a good deal of sensitivity towards women.)

This woman, says Jesus, showed much love; earlier it was suspect love, but now it is true love, though with the same dedication of heart and spirit. I know that since Luther's doctrine of 'justification by grace alone' (which is what the three readings are about today) dozens of books have been written about the question whether God's grace takes the sinner unawares or God's own heart is affected by seeing so much love in a person. Quite apart from all the learned reflection on this, I do not see any contradiction here: the fact is that Jesus is taken by surprise by the experience of so much dedicated love on the part of this woman (Luke here even speaks of the 'diakonia' of the woman; even here the real origin of this story has not completely disappeared).

Can God who is in a unique way present in this man Jesus not himself be moved by the goodness and service which people sometimes show amidst all the meaninglessness? Of course this is a *reaction* of a human being, a woman, to what and who Jesus really was. The theological priority of grace is maintained in this context. But can we, through Luke's story, forget Jesus' happy surprise at what this woman, through her anointing and tears, did for him? People can also amaze God! Perhaps this is our greatest thanks and praise to the one whom we may stammeringly call God and whose name really means 'the one who loves humankind'.

8

We want to see Jesus

(John 12.20-32)

At the word of welcome

In the first reading, from Jeremiah, we hear that God is going to renew again with all creation in Christ Jesus the covenant that he made with all creation and afterwards renewed in a special way with the Jewish people, a covenant which was infringed by human beings both in respect of the creation and in respect of the people of God. All this is related to what we now call 'the conciliar process'.

The Gospel according to John

'Now among those who went up to worship at the feast were some Greeks. So these came to Philip, who was from Bethsaida in Galilee, and said to him, "Sir, we wish to see Jesus." Philip went and told Andrew; Andrew went with Philip and they told Jesus. And Jesus answered them, "The hour has come for the Son of man to be glorified. Truly, truly, I say to you, unless a grain of wheat falls into the earth and dies, it remains alone; but if it dies, it bears much fruit. He who loves his life loses it, and he who hates his life in this world will keep it for eternal life. If anyone serves me,he must follow me; and where I am, there shall my servant be also; if any one serves me, the Father will honour him"' (John 12.20-26).

Homily

In those days the approach of Passover, the great feast of the Jews, did not affect just the Jews. In mixed societies one group joins in celebrating the festivals of the others. Festivals have their own dynamics; they make men and women brothers and sisters, even when they think differently or believe differently. For example, not everyone who has a decorated Christmas tree at home is commemorating the birth of Jesus; 1 May is not a workers' festival for everyone who celebrates it. Festivals are not just an invitation to join in the celebrations but also an occasion for asking deeper questions. That is the case with some Greeks, non-Jews, in today's story from the Gospel of John.

Jesus is in Jerusalem for the celebration of the feast of the passover, in fact his last. Some Greeks ask Philip not so much to be able to talk with Jesus; the literal text is 'to see Jesus'. In the Fourth Gospel 'seeing' means the beginning of possible faith. These Greeks, probably proselytes, i.e. Gentiles who are friendly to the Jews and who have begun to celebrate the passover with them, want to know who Jesus really is. In the Gospel of John the answer to such questions is always 'Come and see.' Philip and Andrew tell Jesus about the question of these Greeks. This time Jesus answers rather abruptly: 'The hour has come for the Son of man to be glorified... Unless a grain of wheat falls into the earth and dies, it remains alone; but if it dies, it bears much fruit.'

The narrative context seems remote here. Some Greeks, non-Jews, want to see Jesus, but in answer to their request Jesus begins to speak of his crucifixion. Where is the meaningful connection here? It is as if no notice had been taken of the question of the Greeks. But Jesus' answer takes up the religious quest of these Greeks directly: according to the Gospel of John it is only through his death that Jesus becomes important for the Gentiles. Jesus' glorification makes him universally accessible. At his death Jesus will 'draw all to him' (John 12.32), including the Gentiles. For John, to see Jesus means to believe that through the sacrifice of his life Jesus is glorified with the Father, from where he also provides access to the Father for all men and women who follow him in service along this way of life.

What we have here is no longer an encounter of Greeks with the historical Jesus, but a decision about the exalted Christ. And for John the exaltation of Jesus is completed on the cross. That is the paradox of the Christian faith. For Jesus and also for us consummation appears in the form of a fiasco.

We can understand such texts ideologically and quite perversely, as though people who are poor, needy and unsuccessful on earth can find their consolation in a later heavenly life. In a world in which the hopelessness of the poor majority can no longer be overlooked by the over-satisfied minority the first question is whether there is a basis for hope in life before death; only then can the question of life after death also be raised meaningfully. A church which lives with a message that contains the promise of life even after death will do well to take life before death with radical seriousness: the content of the life of human beings, animals and the earth. The credibility of a further hope reaching beyond death is also decided in and through the openness of Christians to the earthly hope of their fellow human beings, to justice and peace already realized in a world made whole.

John's story is not about good advice from the followers of Jesus to others who find things difficult and are burdened; here there is no detached talk about others. The story is about the specific conditions of this discipleship for anyone who will listen to Jesus. And the answer is clear: 'Whoever loves his life will lose it'; 'Anyone who wants to serve me must follow in my footsteps.' The background is the dialectical tension between 'life on earth' and 'eternal life' which embraces all being. The bond in this dialectic is the cross in the form of sacrifice. Not suffering for the sake of suffering, but suffering as the historically unavoidable complement to our dedication for righteousness and peace and our opposition to the devastation of God's creation. Between the world, human beings and God there is always a mediation, even in the negative, namely in sin. Sin certainly wounds God, but it affects God *in* his creatures: in human beings and in the world of creation in which they share, in animals and plants, in their and our natural milieu, in our society, in our hearts, our innermost being and our presence in solidarity with our fellow human beings. From a theological perspective, to hurt and damage this world is a sin against the Creator of heaven and earth – against the one whom under whatever name many people call God: the mystery that has the passion for the 'wholeness' of nature and world history, of society and human beings among one another.

Those who oppose injustice and evil in a world in which much evil brings about and establishes injustice and dedicate themselves to the good and to justice will be persecuted. But despite opposition, torture and even death, this dedication has *life* in itself, a life that is stronger than death. There are radical texts in the New Testament which can make us uncomfortable. There are also other, consoling texts in the New Testament in which we can read that being a Christian is also a possibility for mediocre and anxious people. But this text of John does not belong with them: here we have an indication of the radical character of being a follower of Jesus. Few of us are 'all-or-nothing' types. Therefore now and then we must be confronted with the radical aspects of the gospel. Saints who put this gospel radicalism into practice are like the tip of the iceberg; they are the best of the mass of ice which itself remains invisible under water – we mediocre ones! – *they* are peaks where the Christian faith becomes visible to the world in its utmost authenticity and where the world is already healed, as an example and hope for all of us.

The great drama of 'life here' and 'life there, in the hereafter' is not simply staged as an intimate performance for the individual soul. The theme of life here and eternal life is indissolubly bound up with the great words 'assembly' and 'community', and thus with peace. That becomes clear where the gospel speaks about the grain of wheat which does not remain alone but bears much fruit. The contrast which is made here is not just the contrast between dying, perishing and coming to be, but also that between 'remaining alone' or 'bearing fruit'. Evidently in the end what is involved is more than a matter of life *before* and life *after* death; what is at stake is also life in solitude or life in community; abandonment or love. Any community has the chance, through the love and fellowship experienced in its own circles, to become a sign *of life* for others.

Only if our community is such a community of love, will Greeks, outsiders to the Albertinum, come to say, 'We want to see Jesus', we want to enquire more deeply into who you really are. One can exist physically, even in prosperity and in a comradely group, and at the same time be hopelessly alone. And one can die with the hope of a rich harvest and a full community. Perhaps we can learn from our mediocrity and anxiety to live with the more radical perspectives of our Christian faith. That, on this Sunday in Lent, is the message of the Gospel of John for us.

9

'Apocalypse Now'
(Matthew 24.37-45)

At the word of welcome

During last week [this was in 1983] many people in the Netherlands were frightened by a radio interview with a man who forecast the end of the world for Thursday 1 December 1983. After it the telephone at the broadcasting station was red hot. Rumour had it that according to this prophet, a spaceship was also ready, to offer some of the elect a chance to escape the catastrophe. All this was told me by a taxi-driver. Afterwards I too heard a whole discussion over the radio about whether it was sensible of the radio station to broadcast such a panic interview.

What struck me about the taxi-driver was that he himself said: 'Fancy that! a space ship – like Noah's ark in the old days'. That is also the beginning of today's reading, 'As in the days of Noah'.

Homily

Given the spontaneous reaction of this taxi-driver, today's reading from Matthew is obviously one form of a deeply human story of all times, constantly new. Not only social and economic crises but also cosmic events, when otherwise peaceful nature becomes turbulent, in the form of earthquakes, hurricanes and large-scale floods, periodically arouse apocalyptic agitation among human beings. In view of the threat of the death of the principles of life in our system, above all in view of the threat of nuclear warheads almost next to our homes, a time also of social unrest and deep malaise in the church, our time, too, is ripe for apocalyptic panic.

'Apocalypse Now' was the title of a recent film; this could also have been the title of the Matthaean pericope from today's liturgy. That is what it was also like in the days of Noah: also in the days of Isaiah, as the first reading says – when the northern kingdom had fallen and even Jerusalem was threatened. That is also what it was like in the time of Jesus. That is what it was like in the time of

Augustine, in the transition from the world of late antiquity to the Western period. And that is what it was like at the transition from the autumn of the Middle Ages to our modern times. Luther thought that the end of the times was very near, and he saw the fact that the Elbe had then burst its banks as the greatest sign of the end of the world. Biblical and later history clearly point to deeply engrained universal human models, a possible ground on the one side for hope and on the other for thoughts of doom.

What has all this to do with our Christian faith?

We modern men and women confront such phenomena in a very matter-of-fact way. We know 'better'. And yet! The short reading from Matthew seems to me to be meant specifically for matter-of-fact, as it were secularized people, like us. In chs.24 and 25 Matthew collects divergent pieces of tradition from different periods about the end of 'this world' and works it all into a whole, as specific catechesis for his community. In the first part of this chapter reference is made to apocalyptic agitation, and in opposition to these grim rumours, Matthew summons his community to sobriety and calm: you must not run after all these false prophets who forecast the end of the world. For Matthew it is certain that this end is in fact on the way, but when it comes it will be quite clear to everyone: there is no need to try to read it off some magic crystal ball. People are therefore to be sober and critical in the face of all kinds of adventitious rumours.

But in the second half of this chapter, the part that was read out, Matthew is clearly concerned with quite a different situation of the Chrsitian community of faith. The community already knows the *déja vu*, the old story of the end which is coming very soon, of which many credulous people have become the dupes. Scepticism has set in. People have as it were seen through the model, and so it has lost its dynamic force. Now, says Matthew, there is no longer any talk of an imminent apocalypse. Some Christians have become completely indifferent to it. They no longer think of a possible end, as the language and expresion of God's final judgment. They live their everyday life in an ordinary way: they eat and drink, sleep and marry, work in the fields or grind corn – all good things in themselves. For in contrast to the other Gospels Matthew says nothing about the biblical recollection of the immoral behaviour of many people in the days of Noah, which had led to the flood.

Matthew is not at all concerned with 'this evil generation' but with (to put it in modern terms) 'secularized Christians', who perhaps live good lives, but *etsi Deus non daretur*, as though there were no longer any question of God. They lack religious depth. Sober apocalyptic tension seems to belong at the heart of Christianity. That emerges from two examples which Matthew gives. Two men are doing the same work in the field; two women are also doing the same thing, namely grinding corn or wheat. But at the coming of the Lord for the last judgment, one man and one woman may go with the Coming One and enter the kingdom of God, while the other man and the other woman are left behind in their field and at their grinding. There is nothing here about an arbitrary election or predestination by God. The key word of this pericope is 'active watchfulness'. Matthew goes on to fill out the details of what this active watchfulness means in the sequel to this and in the following chapter. Watchfulness there means faithfully fulfilling the task one has been given (Matt.24.45/25.30), and here Matthew himself gives the criteria on the basis of which we shall be judged: it will be by the criterion of our concern for the smallest, the least among us.

In place of apocalyptic agitation and thoughts of doom, in place also of a soberly human, indifferent worldly life, in Matthew Jesus says that God is certainly and inevitably coming, but that this coming-to-judgment cannot be dated. This judgment is only a deadly apocalyptic threat for us if we fail to look round carefully every day at our fellow human beings and only play our role in the daily social process. In the Gospel of Matthew, remaining awake and watchful quite clearly means being attentive to your fellow human beings, concerned for them: for particular poor, hungry, oppressed and outcast people. Even the Son does not know the hour. So here horoscopes are completely of the evil one.

The only correct and adequate answer to the question which was put on all sides in Jesus' time and which in the New Testament the disciples had also put to Jesus, 'Lord, when is the end coming, and what are the signs of it?', is therefore: do not puzzle over such things, but live an ordinary life as Christians, in accordance with the practice of the kingdom of God; then no one and nothing can come upon you unexpectedly apart from the liberating rule of God himself.

Apocalyptic agitation is certainly of the evil one, but so too is religious indifference: true expectation of the end in faith is doing the works of the kingdom of God. It does not matter whether you are now working in the field or grinding corn, whether you are a priest or a professor, a cook or a porter, or just an old age pensioner. What matters is how your life looks when you hold it up to the light of the gospel of the God whose nature is to love humankind. That decides whether you will be left behind bereft and alone at your grinding or in the field; whether you do not go along, and disappear from the joy of God and human happiness for good.

As we meditate on this pericope from Matthew this year we are at the beginning of Advent: the liturgical New Year. The alpha, or the beginning, seems to derive its sense from meditation on the end, the omega of our life. Anyone who wants to make a good beginning must keep the end in view: not the end that we ourselves want to reach as athletes with our own trained strength, but an end-point that looks promising, that attracts us and invites us encouragingly, as an undeserved greater future for those who are in fact also concerned to make a future for their fellow human beings here in this world. For us it is like being a child learning to walk: like father and mother in a young family walking beside their baby and encouraging its first steps, with their four arms stretched out on all sides (in obvious concern for the child), almost dancing in the process. Baby's little legs have to be able to work by themselves, but without all these stretching and welcoming arms the baby would never be able to venture alone. That is '*adventus Domini*', the coming to us of God in all our history and above all in the man Jesus, the Christ.

10

Zeal for God's house has consumed me

(John 2.13-25)

At the word of welcome

In fact there is a degree of arbitrariness or chance in the choice of readings by our liturgists. Whether it is deliberate or not, there is an enormous tension between the first reading from Exodus and the second reading about the cleansing of the temple, particularly in its Johannine version. The story of the first three evangelists is gentler, more friendly to the Jews; here we have the voice of temple reformers with accusations of misuse. But in the exclusivist Gospel of John Jesus contrasts all temples and synagogues, pagodas, mosques and church buildings with the new temple, and that is the dead but risen Jesus Christ.

Homily

In today's first reading (Exodus 20.1-17) the Ten Words, better known to us as the 'Commandments', are offered us as a guideline for our lives. The meaning of each of the ten guidelines is: 'I, God, am the only One.' That does not mean: 'I, God, am *everything*', for alongside God there are also other beings, above all living, real people, about whom there are the many other Words. There is only one God, but this God is a God *of human beings*, a God who wants to venture with human beings, regardless of how trustworthy or untrustworthy they are. He risks this. In the second reading, the story of the cleansing of the temple, it is clear that for Jesus, too, and above all, God is 'the only one', but he is the only one precisely in his dealings with human beings for human happiness – in a cosmos made whole (Ex.20.10, in one of its Ten Words, calls for rest on the sabbath for our animals as well!).

Since our childhoods and the devotional pictures we had then, we have had a vivid idea of the cleansing of the temple. In them Jesus looked like a modern squatter. All four of the Gospels have this story. But today we are confronted with the *Johannine* version of a more original story to which differing theological significance is given in the four views of the one gospel. The particular interpretation of the Gospel of John is striking. Alongside features which it has in common with the other three Gospels there are clear differences and peculiarities in this Gospel. First of all the Gospel of John puts this event right at the beginning of Jesus' public ministry, whereas the three other Gospels have it taking place at the end of that ministry, just before the passion narrative: they see it as the chief motive for Jesus' arrest. Moreover this scene (and this is the point in John) is immediately connected with a saying of Jesus about the destruction of the temple and the rebuilding of it in a short time, in three days.

In Jesus' time, probably as a result of a recent decision by the high priest Caiaphas, for the first time cattle and sheep were admitted to the outermost part of the temple, which was also open to non-Jews (the so-called 'Court of the Gentiles'), to be sold for temple sacrifices: before that they could only be bought in the market near the Mount of Olives, though that was close by. This fact bears witness to the growing corruption of the temple priests under the Roman occupation. All this also involved the activity of moneychangers, because according to Jewish law coins with the image of the Roman emperor on them could not be used in the sacred precincts of the temple; that is where the bank was kept. The temple priests, who collaborated with the Romans, devised a procedure. The money was changed for shekels, a transaction in which the moneychangers made a profit. It is striking that the other three Gospels speak only of doves – these were the offering of *poor* people. However, John also has masses of cattle and sheep present in the forecourt of the temple; moreover they get the worse treatment. Jesus deals more gently with those who sell doves: they are simply asked to leave the forecourt with these doves. The sacrificial animals *of the rich* are swept out by Jesus.

I think that we must distinguish two levels of meaning in this story. On the one hand, what drove Jesus to his action? What was his motive and what could the bystanders make of his intervention? And on the other hand, how did the evangelists understand this story theologically, each from his own perspective, and develop it further in the light of the later death and resurrection of Jesus? In other words, what did this event mean for anyone who saw it and took part in it? And what does it mean in the later theology of the New Testament? Both versions have a message for us.

Protest against profanations of God's house, the temple, was already an old prophetic tradition in Israel; in that protest there also lived on the expectation that an eschatological cleansing of the temple was on the way. In John the miracle of Cana immediately precedes the cleansing of the temple. Just as in Cana a superabundance of wine is present as a sign of the coming of messianic times, so in the messianic time the temple will be completely purified, hallowed, indeed replaced by the true worship 'in spirit and truth' which will take place neither in the temple of Jerusalem nor in the Samaritan sanctuary on Mount Gerizim, as the chapter which follows the story of the cleansing of the temple says (John 4).

So Jesus' action stands in an Old Testament tradition from which there is also abundant quotation by the four Gospels. The prophet Jeremiah already rebuked the temple priests of his time because they allowed the temple to become a 'den of thieves', a robbers' cave (Jer.7.11, cited by Mathew and Mark), and here he prophesied that God would destroy the temple of Jerusalem as he had formerly destroyed the sanctuary of Shiloh. That had since happened. And after the exile we find in Zechariah (14.21) the image of the ideal temple in which everything will be 'holy': you can go there with your everyday pots and bowls; holy vessels are no longer needed; everything in Israel is sanctified; and 'temple merchants' will no longer be found there (the Gospel of John alludes to this). In Malachi (3.1) there is mention of a coming of the Lord to the temple after a strict chastising of the misdeeds of the Levitical temple servants. And finally the prophet Isaiah 56.7 (cited by Luke 19.26) points to the ideal of a temple as a 'perfect house of prayer' on the holy mountain of Zion, which will draw all peoples to it.

But there is more in the Gospel of John than all these biblical recollections. For the people with whom Jesus dealt and who witnessed his appearance in the temple were not so familiar with the Bible that they could recall all these biblical texts! They heard these old prophecies only as they were reflected by what was experienced here and now among an oppressed people. In this time of occupation the people were furious about the temple rulers, and also about the temple which had become a political stronghold, where the temple priests exploited the people in cowardly, obedient collaboration with the Romans. But the believing people still went each year *en masse* to the temple, and for them it was still the abode of the Lord.

However, we know from the rabbinic literature that already in the year 30, i.e. during Jesus' lifetime, there were believing Jews who for a period undertook a special fast so that the Jerusalem temple might be spared. And according to Flavius Josephus, a pro-Roman Jewish historian of this time, in the year 62, eight years before the destruction of the temple at the time of the Jewish war, there was a certain Jesus bar Ananias who made a fierce public attack on the temple and warned of a coming destruction of it as a punishment from God. First of all there were Jewish, not Christian intimations of the destruction of the temple in the year 70! The political situation of the time everywhere aroused the sorry expectation of a new destruction of the temple of Jerusalem.

Jesus of Nazareth also stands in the same context. His modest gesture of suddenly making cords into a brush or scourge and for a moment giving short shrift to those in the temple as it were crystallized the wrath of the people against the temple priests of the time who oppressed them. The anger and wrath of the tormented and exasperated people burst out in an explosion of holy wrath in this appearance of Jesus. The deepest meaning of the Torah, the law as the will of God, had become a mockery of the One God in his one relation to all his downtrodden people. All this drove Jesus to his historic appearance in the Temple. Caiaphas, the high priest, in particular had understood this well; he was behind the plot against Jesus.

But the Gospel of John introduces a second dimension. Jesus does not just drive out the animals: he drives out the animal *sacrifices*. In the Gospel of John his criticism of the temple is radical. Along with the circle around Stephen in Jerusalem, the Letter to the Hebrews, the Qumran hymns, etc. this Gospel stands in a very Jewish way in a tradition clearly hostile to the temple. Only in John is the original scene which can still be detected in the Gospel of John connected, after Jesus' resurrection, with Psalm 69.9: 'Zeal for your house has consumed me'. In John this becomes: 'Zeal for the temple will consume me', i.e. it will destroy me completely: the destruction of the temple here is the death of Jesus, just as the rebuilding of the new temple in three days points to the rising again of Jesus as the Christ, the one who is raised from the dead.

In the theological dimension of this story of John there is no longer any mention of the Jerusalem temple, first of all because the Jewish temple had by then long been destroyed, namely in the year 70, but above all because in the Gospel of John Jesus himself from the beginning is the temple or the presence of God among us: 'He has set up his *shekinah*, i.e. his tent or ark, among us'; '*He has dwelt among us*' (John 1.14), as a good English translation has it. Already during his lifetime, but above all through his death, the Risen Christ is the true temple as a result of which the Jerusalem temple has lost its historical and religious significance. The context of Psalm 69.7-9 is important; it reads: 'For it is for your sake that I have borne reproach, that shame has covered my face. I have become a stranger to my brethren, an alien to my mother's sons. For zeal for your house has consumed me, and the insults of those who insult you have fallen upon me.'

According to John 2.12 (in this story just before the event of the cleansing of the temple) Jesus' brothers forsake him; out of unbelief they keep their distance from Jesus during the whole of his ministry.

Thus the prophecy of the destruction of the temple in the Gospel of John means the life and death of Jesus, which is not understood by his family; and the rebuilding of the temple is related to his resurrection. Jesus' zeal for the true worship of God, which does not oppress poor men and women but raises them up, was the end of him, but God himself vindicated this despised figure by his resurrection. That is the deepest significance of John's view of this cleansing of the temple; the place of the temple has now been taken by Jesus, and where two or three are gathered together in his name, there is the temple, there is the church, there is Christ. Therefore Jesus has the authority to cleanse the temple of both animals and sacrifice. He is the sacrifice. 'More than Solomon and his temple is here.'

When we hear this story we spontaneously put ourselves on the side of Jesus in his conflict with the temple priests. But this story should also be able to put us church Christians on the other side. Has not our church again become a fortified temple, almost a new stronghold, from which the prophetic breath has disappeared, where God's praise may indeed be sung but where people are trampled under foot? Has not the fetish of doctrine and the fortified logic of orthodoxy taken the place of the cattle and sheep of Jerusalem, though this time human beings are made sacrifical animals? Do we not need a new cleansing of the temple?

Of course, we ourselves, grass-roots believers, *are the church*. We are indeed, but meanwhile there *is* its top, and it is our top, the ministerial part of our native church. Jesus stood on the side of the grass roots, in conflict with the top of his native Israel. Do we still have the fantasy of quickly making a brush out of a few cords, as Jesus did? Sometimes I feel aggressive, sometimes cowardly, but *never discouraged*. Time itself erodes any glorious powerful manifestation of any world power – whether state or church. Defensible but vulnerable and wounded powerlessness is infinitely stronger than all power. The future of our church lies in its active presence in the future of the world, in the future of human beings, above all those who no longer know a future: wounded, oppressed and abandoned people, lonely and unemployed – without forgetting the 'healthy sheep' (Ezekiel 34.16).

May these forty days of fasting be a time in which at least in our own hearts and within our own small-scale surroundings we bring purification, where perhaps in one way or another we drive out a handful with cattle and sheep, or perhaps, in our middle-class way, just... doves. Amen.

11

Transition from Jesus to the church's confession

(John 14.1-12)

At the word of welcome

The Gospel of John, from which today's reading is taken, really gives an explanation of what the first reading from I Peter says about 'the priestly people of God', that we all together form.

Homily

No one can deny from his or her own experience that much wisdom, goodness and truth can be found in our world outside Christ, or outside people who believe in him. And yet we have just heard from the scripture reading that Jesus alone is the way to truth which leads to authentic life: 'I am the way, the truth and the life'; in other words, 'I am the way which leads to true living.' We sometimes have difficulty with this forthright saying.

Many religions have long called themselves 'the way', and have had larger or smaller vehicles for travelling it. In the Acts of the Apostles the movement around Jesus, Christianity, is originally repeatedly called 'the way' – that is the claim of all religions. But in the Gospel of John more than in the other Gospels (which moreover are also written on the basis of a confession of faith) there is something special. Here a person, the man Jesus, one of us, is called in absolute terms 'the way'. There are also other ways, but here this man is confessed as *the* way, no more and no less. The true way of life is shown, not by a particular religious doctrine, not even by a Sermon on the Mount, nor by the outline of a religious programme that must be solemnly observed, but by a person: the person Jesus *is* the way. 'You believe in God, believe also in me', the Gospel of John makes Jesus say.

The reading to which we have just listened makes us think of the story of Moses. In Deuteronomy 1.29-33 we read: 'Do not be afraid. The Lord your God is going before you.' 'The Lord, your God, is going before you to seek you out a place to pitch your tents.' In the

Gospel of John Jesus, the new Moses and liberator, also goes before his followers: in search of places for his disciples to live in. 'I go before you to prepare a place for you' (John 14.2). Like Moses, out in the lead with God, in search of an appropriate camping place for his people on the way from the exodus, so Jesus goes steadfastly forward; he goes away to prepare an appropriate place for his disciples. Therefore it is good that Jesus goes away.

This story is part of what is called Jesus' farewell discourse, and it occurs in that part of the Gospel in which Jesus is no longer speaking openly to 'the world' but in a closed circle to 'his own', his followers. He tells them that he is going away, but he is going *in order to do something* for his disciples. He is going, like Moses, to look for a space where many tents can be pitched for his followers, and in many different styles: 'In my father's abode there is room for many' (John 14.1).

Later in this Gospel we hear that after his departure Jesus is sending his Spirit as an Easter gift: '*On that day* (i.e. on Easter day) I shall come to you and make my abode with you' (John 14.23). Here the old expectation of Moses and his people is fulfilled: the promise of 'God's dwelling among humankind' (e.g. Exod.25.8; 29.45). The place of God's presence among humankind is no longer the tent of the covenant, the ark, nor the temple in Jerusalem or Mount Gerizim. It is the believers themselves, the community of God. What originally only Jesus, himself the temple of the holy Spirit, could do and indeed did, can be done by all Christians after the Easter experience. Therefore Jesus says: 'You shall do greater things than I', all Christians. Wherever Christians appear they must do what Jesus did, and they *can* do it, in the power of the Spirit and therefore after prayer. Like Jesus they now themselves put others on the way of truth which leads to life.

How can that be? Formerly Moses asked God, 'Show us your glory' (your *kabod* or majesty). Now Philip asks Jesus: 'Show us the Father.' In Jesus' reply the Gospel of John really points towards the prologue of this Gospel: 'We have seen his glory, the glory of the only Son of the Father' (John 1.14). Hence 'Philip, whoever sees me, sees the Father' (John 14.9). Moses saw only *the back* of God who in the meantime passed by unnoticed, invisibly. By contrast, Jesus' followers see in one man, Jesus, God's glory as it were in the human face. So he or she knows the way; it is to follow the footsteps of Jesus in good days and in bad. Nowhere does the Gospel tell us what truth and life are, to what Jesus is the way. Here there is no Sermon on the Mount; there are no religious guidelines: only a human Someone who says 'Live from God' and therefore is himself also love, but goes away. If Jesus becomes your way, then any fellow human being whom you encounter is a challenge and a call; in him or her Jesus stands before you as someone who needs you. To follow the life of Jesus in this way is to seek God. And anyone who does that will come to truth and life, whatever this may also mean: 'Do not be afraid. You believe in God, believe also in me.' What a simple and clear Gospel that of John is, although it seems so complicated and from another world! But you must read this Gospel along with the first three Gospels as it were to provide 'historical background'.

'John' composed his Gospel with the figure of Moses and his history (as these were current in the Jewish Moses mysticism of Jesus' day) in view. But, John says, 'The law is given by Moses, but grace and truth came through Jesus Christ' (John 1.17). Here is a greater than Moses and all the other prophets. Of course this Gospel knows as well as our own experience tells us that we are all often tempted in this faith – that we are surprised at our own faith despite doubt. In the Gospel of John Jesus asks seriously, 'Will you too go away?', whereupon the disciples reply just as seriously, 'To whom shall we go?' Either you let yourself fall into the emptiness and darkness of your finite existence or you believe in a mystery which cannot be put into words, which embraces you and never lets you go: God, as many religions show him, and above all Jesus as a full-length portrait in sharper contours, as a living human figure.

Moreover we learn from Jesus that we will never be deceived, even if our way goes through crucifixion. The abyss of this incomprehensible world is not deeper nor more real than the abyss of God's mystery that in Jesus shows us the form of love, of mercy and of promise. That today is the message of the reading from the Gospel of John.

II · The Confession of Jesus in the Church

12

Christmas meditation: 'Being made man'

(Matthew 2.13-21)

Homily

In the days when Rabbi Menahem lived in the land of Israel it came about that a crazy man climbed a high mountain unnoticed and from the top of the mountain blew a trumpet over the whole city. Among the excited people the rumour quickly went the rounds: 'That was the trumpet announcing our liberation.' When the rumour also came to the ears of Rabbi Menahem, he went to the window; he opened it and looked at the world outside. Somewhat sadly and gruffly he then muttered: 'What I see is no renewal.'

At the birth of Jesus there was just as little that was special to see through the window of the world. Outside the later Gospels, only a couple of secular Roman historians of the time document in passing mention at most the name of Jesus. In this respect the Christmas story of Matthew 2.13-31 is even bewildering. At Jesus' birth there was a bloodbath among the newborn children. Since nowadays we hear repeatedly via television or other news media of bloodbaths in one place or another, we read this story from a different perspective from before. Then we forgot the bloodbath and were glad that Jesus escaped it. Now this massacre of children oppresses us. Whether this bloodbath and the flight to Egypt associated with it are historical or not is not really the point. What matters is what the text – however it came into being – wants to tell us about the birth of Jesus, long after his death.

Matthew says that because of the one whom Christians call the coming saviour and liberator, innocent children were murdered, while the baby Jesus was spared. From a human perspective this is quite bewildering, above all if we connect it with another story from the Gospels: 'It is better that one man should die for the whole people' (John 18.14). In Matthew's story Herod has 'all the young boys of two years and under murdered' (Matt.2.16). Historically speaking, we know that he was quite capable of doing this. According to the story he was afraid of losing his royal power to 'king Jesus'. The incarnation of Jesus provoked a bloodbath. Later, things get even worse. History bears witness that there is no part of our earth where Western Christians, often in the name of Jesus, have not brought about devastation, destroying peoples and cultures, which these people now painfully point out. Better not to believe in God than in a God who enslaves and diminishes human beings.

These are not very nice thoughts, and some people may think them inappropriate thoughts for Christmas – a day on which according to ancient custom in domestic, protected security and peace, at a time when everything in nature is frozen, withered and brown, we all bring green into our houses as a sign of life and hope, despite our experience to the contrary, perhaps in order to forget this contrary. But Matthew's Christmas story directs us to a more cruel world; a world in which nature and history are indissolubly interwoven and in this weaving together show a side to which no one can be reconciled.

We are forced to speak of fundamental 'negative experiences of contrast'. The basic 'pre-religious' experience accessible to all human beings lies in the human rejection of the world which is *as it is*. What we experience as reality, what we also see and hear every day through television and other mass media is evidently not in order: something is basically wrong there. Reality is full of contradictions. Therefore the human experience of suffering, evil and misfortune is the basis and source of the fundamental veto of human beings to the fact of our being in the world. Moreover, this experience is clearer and more evident than any 'knowledge' that philosophy and science can give us. Indignation seems to be the basic experience of our life in this world. This is not a cheerful thought on Christmas Day. But for most people this is not a *thought* at all, but an experience which they cannot escape. That is our world... unless we run blindly through the world, bent only on consumption, bustle and oblivion.

Without doubt there is also a good deal of goodness and beauty, much to enjoy in this world. The good is even older than the evil, which is never original except for a dualist. There even seems to be more joy and singing to hear among oppressed people than among their grim oppressors. But all these fragments of goodness, beauty and meaning are constantly opposed and countered by evil and hatred, by blatant or dull suffering, by power and terror. This contradiction, which is characteristic of our world, makes both evil and good mutually indifferent. And so human indignation continues incessantly. It is not the sign of a decadent life that no longer finds anything worth living or dying for. In the end human beings reject evil on the basis of a comparison with good. In the meantime, however, in our world there is that constantly puzzling mixture of good and evil, of meaning and meaninglessness.

We do not know from history what will get the upper hand in this mixture, nor even whether there is a last word at all.

One positive element in this fundamental experience of contrast is invincible human indignation at injustice and innocent suffering. Not being able to succumb to the situation offers an illuminating perspective. In it there is *openness to* another situation, which has a claim to our affirmative yes, a consensus with 'the unknown', the content of which cannot even be defined positively: another, better world which in fact we do not find anywhere. This is openness to the unknown. The radical experience of a veto discloses a yes without content which is therefore open, just as immovable as the human no and perhaps stronger, because this open yes is the basis for opposition to the negative. Moreover, from time to time there are fragmentary but real experiences of meaning and happiness, on a smaller or larger scale, which constantly refuel, support and maintain this open yes. Here those who believe in God and agnostics are in accord, and on the basis of this there is sufficient basis for solidarity of all with all. For their part believers fill in the basic experience in a 'religious' way; through this the open yes gets direction and perspective, not so much (at least directly) from the inexpressible divine transcendence which cannot be put into words as from the recognizable 'human face' of this transcendence as it appeared among us in the man Jesus. The fundamental murmuring thus becomes well-founded hope. There is something of a sigh for mercy in reality. Those who believe in God hear in this the breath of God's saving creation with a view to more humanity in the world!

Have we meanwhile diverged from our theme of Christmas as a festival of incarnation? 'The word became human' (John 1.14). The anonymity of God's invisible face takes on human features and therefore features that we can recognize. In Matthew's Christmas story it becomes clear that Jesus becomes truly man, without any condition, without any claim to even a suspicion of divine attributes for his humanity. God discloses *his being in the humanity* of Jesus. He becomes man in this our disputed world, which we cannot accept as it is. In Matthew's account it immediately appears that as someone from Nazareth Jesus is a stranger in Bethlehem. All doors are closed to him; he is born in a manger. Matthew makes Jesus' end, as one who is outcast and rejected, already begin at his birth. The Son of man comes into a world in which 'Auschwitz' and 'Hiroshima' are constant possibilities again and indeed keep happening, into a world which allows millions of children to die of hunger every year. To become human is to come into this world, even for Jesus.

Therefore the incarnation of Jesus is fundamental opposition to this world. But in the coming of Jesus the fundamental, open yes becomes a clear message; only more humanity, to the end, can save the world. The open yes which, because it has no contours, gets hidden in our human protest, takes on concrete contours in Jesus. That will emerge later in his activity. He proclaims in every kind of tone, and fulfils what he proclaims tangibly through his action and his whole way of life. He gives perspective on how the human face of the world can look; he treads the way to it before us. From this it emerges that he believes in a God who wholly accepts human beings as they are and tries to renew them, on the basis of this unmerited acceptance, in relation to themselves and to others in a world that human beings can live in, although the actual world will reject Jesus' message along with his person. Rejection is always the actual state of so many people. And does he not become ***human***?

In our human world of intrinsic contradiction there seems to be no place for true, good humanity. Where this comes into being, it is pelted with stones by this world, sometimes even by churches and religions in it. Humanity is too threatening for the powerful; it reveals their weak spot, their vulnerability and ultimate helplessness. Their power which crushes people and structurally forces their backs to the wall is really disguised powerlessness which, precisely because it is powerless, arms itself with terror and annihilation, with torture and even with nuclear weapons, with a Herod-like massacre of children.

Through his message and his way of life Jesus redefines in word and deed what being human is and what being God means. And he does this by declaring humanity to be the nature of God. According to Jesus there is no difference between what scholars call 'God in himself' and 'God for us'. He is God for us in his own being. In eternal, absolute freedom God himself defines who and what and how he will be in his own divine identity. So the Bible says 'God is love'. It was and is God's free decision to see and define himself as a 'God of human beings', a God 'who loves humankind', identifying himself with vulnerable people who in their vulnerability can also be wounding. Without any privileges he shares our human fate. If we can rightly say of him, 'We too are human beings. Why him and not us?' (H.Oosterhuis), Jesus says equally rightly from his side, 'I too am human. Why you and not me?' You in a stinking stable and not me? You often rejected and not me? Is this incarnation? All the rest is docetism or pseudo-humanity. Here, on extremely sensitive human ground, problems of high christology are involved which in official Christianity are often domesticized by force: what they really mean is tamed and kept down. They then become tamed dogmas which have lost their critical force. Really only those who have suffered, in *person* and in *others*, know what concern for fellow human beings and their society, what concern for more humanity, require of us. 'The word' which in the beginning came to bring order into the primal chaos becomes human: someone who as a human being wants to bring order to things; he wants to remove our chaos in word and deed by radical humanity in our world as a visible form of the all-embracing love of God.

We all dream about the human face of our society and of each individual personally, while cultural historians and analysts paint a somewhat more sombre picture in almost apocalyptic colours. What we see are tortured faces, swollen and emaciated bodies; flies which lick tears from quivering, soiled cheeks. How inhuman and soiled was Jesus' face on the cross? At present stations of the cross are forbidden by the church because of this truth, as though we did not want to know the truth. Only the 'divine radiance and power' are approved of, and that encourages positions of power.

Some people keep getting gentler as they grow older (and in dealings between one person and another that is quite right). As I get older, I myself get increasingly grimmer, or more exactly sadder, about this situation of ours, whether on a small, large or global scale. Is this a world *of God*, revealed as the one who loves humankind?

And yet! Over against all this indignation and sorrow the liberating yes can time and again be heard everywhere, for Christians in a uniquely concentrated way in the career of Jesus. The world certainly puts Christian faith seriously to the test. Disarmed, I can only believe; theoretically not even knowing whether I am on the right track, but convinced that I am remaining intellectually honest. It is certainly here that we have the great human problems.

If not only the world but also the church, which as a part of the world is sometimes more worldly than the world itself, wants to become more human, then the church – i.e. leaders and followers – must first become aware of the nagging experience of suffering humanity and consequently also go through the school of *docta ignorantia*: learning to doubt with the doubters, searching with those who search, suffering with those who suffer, being open to 'the unknown' and not keeping the free Holy Spirit in its own sovereign care. As the people used to complain: where are our 'good shepherds' of old?

On Christmas Day one can howl for one's own church... and yet be a Christian believer. That is Christmas joy, albeit in the minor key. Through that people come closer together than ever. They become a gospel comfort for one another. Is not this, too, 'building the church': a sign for the world, *sacramentum mundi*?

13

Jesus' baptism in the Jordan

'God with us' as obedient son

(Matthew 3.12-17)

At the word of welcome

In today's liturgy we recall the baptism of Jesus in the Jordan. Remarkably, nothing about this baptism has found its way into our Christian confession of faith or our creed, though Jesus' desire to have himself be baptized was nevertheless of fundamental significance for his career or way of life.

Homily

Down the ages the baptism of Jesus by John has caused Christians innumerable difficulties. This Jewish baptism has itself been 'rebaptized' to become the source and foundation of the Christian sacrament of baptism. Nevertheless, the decision by Jesus to go from Nazareth in Galilee to the west bank of the Jordan, there to have himself baptized by a religious enthusiast called John, is one of the most decisive and fundamental moments of his life – a kind of manifesto. On the basis of this firm desire and with a plan for his life which is already settled, Jesus goes to the Jordan to have himself baptized. So in the Gospel of Matthew this baptism is not itself the central event.

In this story Matthew has first related that 'Jerusalem and all Judaea then went out to John the Baptist' (Matt.3.5) and also 'all the region about the Jordan'; in other words, in this Gospel it is imagined that the whole people of Israel is converted and repents. Matthew goes further and says: 'They were baptized... confessing their sins', for 'the kingdom of heaven was at hand' (Matt.3.2).

Jesus, too, goes from Nazareth in Galilee to the Jordan with the express purpose of having himself baptized by John. Jesus' desire to have himself baptized indicates his fundamental solidarity with sinners, the outcasts of the then society. Matthew fiercely attacks the representatives of this society, who cast out sinners and do not have themselves baptized and act as though they were above all sin. Just beforehand he says to the Pharisees and Sadducees in the words of the Baptist, 'You brood of vipers!'

That Jesus introduces himself to John for the penitential baptism of sinners is typical of his whole attitude to life in taking the side of people who do not count, of sinners. Immediately after this baptism he returns to the wilderness and there rejects any suggestion of seeing the coming of the kingdom of God other than as active support for poor and sinful, and therefore outcast, men and women. So this baptism indicates the programme for Jesus' life. In the Gospel of Matthew solidarity with the least, those who do not count, is also the criterion on the basis of which we shall later be judged by the Son of Man, Jesus Christ. That is the heart of the Gospel of Matthew. In the earlier Gospel, that of Mark, the story of Jesus' baptism culminates in the proclamation and installation of Jesus to be the messianic king and Son of God. However, in the Gospel of Matthew such an installation is not mentioned in any way. In the light of the birth narrative in the Gospel of Matthew, the Matthaean communities already believe in the messianic Sonship of Jesus, not just from his birth but from his conception in his mother's womb. However, Mark wants to base the nature of Jesus on his appointment to be Son of God, and according to his perspective that happens at the baptism: in Mark that is the deepest significance of the baptism.

Matthew turns this story of Mark on its head. Matthew is not concerned with the problem that Jesus is in a unique way Son of God, despite the penitential baptism of John which he undergoes with all the people. The Matthaean communities already know that he is Son of God and is so from his conception in his mother's womb. But for these Christians the baptism for the forgiveness of sins then becomes a problem in the case of Jesus. Why does the Son of God have to subject himself to this Baptist who threatens people with damnation and have himself baptized? How can that be reconciled with the Christian confession about Jesus, the Christ, Son of God, our Lord? Hence the insertion, which is peculiar to Matthew, of John's objection to Jesus' desire to have himself baptized by him; Christians expect rather that Jesus should baptize John! However, in Matthew the question is: of what nature must the sonship of Jesus (which has already been confessed in the first chapter of the Gospel) be if this Jesus, who has already been recognized by the Baptist as stronger and mightier, has himself baptized by one who is weaker and less significant?

Strikingly, verses 14 and 15, in which John the Baptist wants to prevent Jesus from being baptized by him, are unknown in the other Gospels; we also find Jesus' reaction to this (and in the sequence of Matthew's Gospel it is the first remark that we hear from Jesus) only in Matthew, and moreover these words sound very Matthaean: 'Let it be so now; for thus it is fitting for us to fulfil all righteousness' (Matt.3.15). In the Gospel of Matthew Jesus 'fulfils all righteousness'. Whereas in places Matthew says of the disciples and Christians that they 'do' righteousness, he says exclusively of Jesus, in the same sentence, that he 'fulfils righteousness', i.e. Jesus does righteousness both fully and in complete obedience. For Matthew, to do or to fulfil all righteousness means not only to observe the Torah but also to do the whole of God's will; for both Jesus and the Jews of his time the penitential baptism of John is simply part of that. In 5.20 Matthew speaks of 'the better righteousness', which is greater than that of the scribes and Pharisees. Matthew says, in other words: people are God's beloved sons if they obey God's will. In this Jesus has gone before us: in this he is our model and image. His way of life is also our way of life.

In the everyday life of the Jews 'obedience' typifies the Jewish definition of sonship: a son needs to obey. That was the case in the family life of the time, as Matthew also knew it. According to Matthew the uniqueness of Jesus' sonship, which had already been confessed by then, shows itself in his obedience to the will of God in the midst of everyday life. In Matthew the proclamation of Jesus' messianic sonship is no enthronement or installation of Jesus as Son of God, as it still is in Mark, but God's answer to a human life of obedient childlike trust in the will of God. Those who obey God's will and make peace, Matthew says in a later chapter, 'will be called sons of God' (Matt.5.9; cf. 5.45). It emerges from their action for righteousness that they are sons of God.

The two key concepts of this Gospel are 'Immanuel', God with us, and being Son of God. And these two are one: the merciful presence of God with us (= Immanuel) shows itself concretely for us in Jesus' human life of obedience. In a human life, faithful to God's will, God's presence in us is shown and at the same time the divine sonship of the man Jesus becomes visible. Matthew wants to impress on the members of his community that the promise of being a child of God is bound up and interwoven with our everyday life of obedience to God. God's promise of being a child of God applies to those who are obedient: they are 'sons of God'. Matthew does not want in any way to indicate that the sonship of Jesus is completely different from our being children of God. He does not know the Johannine interest of the Fourth Gospel, understandable in itself, that seeks to penetrate human events to arrive at an almost immodest view of heavenly dimensions and relationships. Matthew remains closer to us and to our human problems. He wants rather to impress on his believers that the same structure is present in Jesus' obedient career as in our Christian, obedient way of life, following Jesus. That is the way in which God showed and revealed himself in his Son Jesus Christ.

Whereas in the Gospel of Mark the proclamation of divine sonship was addressed directly and exclusively to Jesus himself, in the Gospel of Matthew the heavenly voice becomes more public: it is addressed also to the crowd of people, to the members of Matthew's community: you Christians are children of God to the degree that you fulfil all righteousness, in the steps of Jesus! In Jesus was manifest the sonship of God in and through his obedience as a human being and as a Jew, who recognized a religious awakening in John's Baptist movement and in it traced God's will here and now, and acted accordingly. It is as simple as that. Herein he reveals himself as God's beloved Son. That is at the deepest level the key concept of the whole of the Gospel of Matthew and that Gospel also shows it clearly, by way of a test, in the story which follows, about the three trials or temptations of Jesus. Jesus is the messianic son of God as one who is completely obedient to God's will and therefore desires to be the lesser, rejects magic and worldly power, is willing to be a servant and to that end also lays himself open to mockery in this life, as though it is only through this that the will of God – and that is 'the salvation of humankind' – is realized or fulfilled. As a human being and a Jew stooping to become a servant who is humble and vulnerable and of no account, the prophet Jesus is truly 'the Son of God'. That is the distinctive message of Matthew's christology in this Gospel – then, yesterday and today. Amen.

14

Temptations: Jesus' option in rejecting earthly power

(Matthew 4.1-11)

At the word of welcome

This year the liturgy of the first Sunday in Lent begins with the marvellous story of Jesus' forty-day fast in the wilderness and the attacks already made there on his life's plan. The key question here is: is the first commandment, 'Love God above everything' and your neighbour as oneself, the deepest concern of Jesus or is he looking for something else?

Homily

At Jesus' baptism his divine sonship manifested itself in and through his obedience as a human being to God in the situation of his Jewish humanity. As a Jew he recognized John's Baptist movement as a call to a religious awakening of all Israel; in it he traced the will of God here and now, and he acted accordingly: he had himself baptized. And at the baptism God himself called him 'my beloved Son'. Jesus as God's beloved Son is a key concept throughout the Gospel of Matthew. After this baptism, in this Gospel Jesus is immediately put to the test. The Gospel of Mark seems to know nothing of the nature of the satanic seductions. In Matthew this stay in the wilderness is given dramatic content with three clearly described temptations. Matthew is here concerned with the distinctive Christian content of Jesus' messianic divine sonship, i.e. with a bit of christology. In the scenario of Judaism, above all after the destruction of the temple, and therefore in the time when Matthew was writing his Gospel, these three temptations take on a special emphasis because at that time in Palestine there was a plethora of messianic pretenders (we hear that even from a Jewish historian like Flavius Josephus and also from pagan historians like Tacitus and Suetonius). The first two temptations go back to a Galilean conception that only great, sensational wonders can demonstrate that someone is a son of God.

On the other hand, the third temptation comes more from an apocalyptic background: here we have the world rule of the messianic king understood in a political apocalyptic sense.

Nowhere does it emerge from the structure of the text that these are personal temptations of Jesus – in the sense that Jesus worried about the content he was to give to his messiahship. At all events, Jesus rejects the alternative possibilities offered from outside, forthrightly and without any wavering, as it were with the Bible in his hand. The background of this story about Jesus' temptation is in fact the permanent misleading of the Jewish people itself.

In the scheme of the first Testament *Israel* is 'son of God' *par excellence*. Now in the Gospel of Matthew the career of Jesus is interpreted as an attempt to relive the authentic spiritual experience of Israel. It is about the religious revival of the twelve tribes of Israel. The key saying in this whole story is Deut.8.2: 'And you shall remember all the way which the Lord your God has led you these forty years in the wilderness, that he might humble you, testing you to know what was in your heart, whether you would keep his commandments, or not.' So Jesus is repeating the experience of Israel and must therefore undergo the same trial as the people once did: stay for forty days in the wilderness and share in Israel's experience.

The first temptation presupposes that Jesus is hungry after forty days fasting, as the people in the wilderness once was. The tempter says, 'If you are the Son of God', and connects this sonship with the miracle of the manna. The tempter's suggestion is that Jesus too, as son of God, can turn stones in the wilderness into tasty bread. Perhaps he can, but he rejects any instigation to misuse his messianic power to his own advantage. Being son of God has nothing to do with such grotesque miracle working!

The prophets also bear witness to Israel's constant temptation to boast that it is son of God: this is the background of the second temptation. This people can indeed always trust God, but it often did so with audacious over-confidence, to the effect: 'Nothing can overcome us, the Lord is with us.' Jesus' reaction to this second temptation is a quotation from Deuteronomy 6.16: 'You shall not tempt the Lord your God as you did in Massa.' This is a reference to the event which is related in Exodus 17.7. There we read: 'Moses called the name of the place Massah and Meribah, because of the faultfinding of the children of Israel, and because they put the Lord to the proof by saying, "Is the Lord among us or not?"' To doubt in God's presence with his people is to put God himself to the test, but the presence of God with his people does not give this people any storm-free zones, any immunity to suffering and adversity.

The third temptation also comes from the experience of Israel, in connection with the promise to Israel in Deuteronomy 6.10-15: 'And when the Lord your God brings you into the land which he swore to your fathers, to Abraham, to Isaac and to Jacob, to give you... then take heed lest you forget the Lord... You shall not go after other gods, for the Lord your God is a jealous God.' According to the third temptation, the anti-Christ, as we hear in the second letter to the Christians of Thessalonica (II Thess. 2.8), gets all power from the devil, in diabolical imitation of God who according to Psalm 2.8 gives his Christ or Messiah power over the world. The suggestion by the devil is that Jesus should make himself anti-Christ instead of Christ. He could (according to a particular magical conception of power) misuse his messianic authority for his own glory, like the false messiah Joseph Theudas who, as Moses once did, was said again to have divided the waters of the Jordan (Acts 5.36), or like Simon Magus (Acts 8.9-10), who dared to leap down from a building, there to be caught up by good spirits. These are real stories from early Christianity, which at the time so spoke to the imagination that they were taken up into the Acts of the Apostles. Such events also form the specific context of this story of Jesus' temptations.

From a human point of view something of this kind was indeed also a possibility for the free man Jesus, but in a sovereignly free human way he rejected that perspective, and precisely in so doing revealed himself to be *the* son of God: that is the point of the Gospel of Matthew. This Gospel regards any other understanding of Jesus' divine sonship as being 'of the devil'. Hence the need for the presence of Satan in this story. It is striking that the messianic title Christ (in other words Messiah) is completely absent from the wider tradition from which the story of the temptations comes to Matthew and Luke – a tradition which the Gospel of Mark does not know but which is common to Matthew and Luke: this tradition fiercely rejects any christology of power, so fiercely indeed that this must have existed at this time among some Christians (one does not fight against windmills). In a later chapter Matthew himself warns the Christians against false prophets and messiahs who want to draw attention to themselves through great wonders from which no one has salvation or benefit and in this way demonstrate that they are special emissaries of God, sons of God.

On closer inspection the three temptations essentially amount to the same thing. Being son of God means showing unconditional loyalty to the first commandment, to love God above everything. To be a son is to show obedience to the Father, as we also heard in the story of Jesus' baptism. Where Israel failed as the son of God, *the* Son succeeded: herein already lies the uniqueness of Jesus of Nazareth as son of God. For Jews and also for Jewish Christians the first words of Israel's great, indeed daily, prayer are in keeping with all this story: 'Hear, O Israel, the Lord our God is one Lord; and you shall love the

Lord your God with all your heart, and with all your soul, and with all your strength' (see Deut.6.4-5). Only the Jew Jesus of Nazareth was found capable of doing that. Therefore he and he alone is *par excellence* '*the* son of God'.

In the story of the temptations the approach of the devil in the first two temptations begins: 'If you are the son of God...' Certainly he is! Then it is suggested to Jesus that he should make use of this sonship to his own advantage, i.e. misuse it. Strikingly, 'if you are the son of God' is no longer used in the third temptation. The seductive suggestion becomes all the more brutal: son of God or not, with my satanic help you can just as well become a child of Satan with a guaranteed absolute rule over the world, in other words, become anti-Christ. We can (regretfully) hardly forget in this connection that in the course of church history Christianity (because of behaviour out of keeping with the gospel) has itself been called anti-Christ. Jesus' temptations remain topical!

We also hear at the crucifixion in Matthew's Gospel: 'If you are the son of God... come down from the cross.' And after the last trial, that of his death, the risen Jesus again ascends a high mountain with his disciples and says there: 'All power is given to me in heaven and on earth' (Matt.28.16-18). The divine counterpart of the devil's suggestion! As the risen one, the powerless and vulnerable earthly Jesus becomes the Lord of history and the world. For Matthew that is ultimately the significance of being 'son of God'. According to this Gospel Jesus wants to restore the relationship of all men and women to God. Jesus is human as men and women must be human in their vulnerable positions, as 'Adam', created in the image of God: a human being as a child of God, and a child of God precisely in being human himself. Jesus does not seek his own will but the will of the Father: that makes him the unique 'messianic son of God'. Therefore we must reflect three times before we speak about the church or the people of God as a 'messianic community'; in that case we must first be subjected to the test of Jesus' three temptations.

Although this story of the three temptations of Jesus, a story of the church and particularly of the gospel, was being told soon afterwards by Christians, the church could rightly speak of Jesus as someone who, as the Letter to the Hebrews was later to put it, 'in every respect has been tempted as we are, yet without sinning' (Heb.4.15b). As one of us, as a man, he goes before us in love of God – for human salvation. Because God was the focus of his whole life, Jesus could also be redeemer and liberator of human beings – all men and women, for God's nature is 'salvation for humankind'. In the story of the three temptations there glows and blossoms that same mysticism of the 'jealous God' from the Jewish tradition of Deuteronomy from which all the scriptural citations in this story of Jesus' temptations come.

'The glory of God is the happiness of living humankind; but the happiness of humankind is the living God.' That is how Irenaeus of Lyons rightly summed up the Christian gospel. The accent on the salvation and happiness of human beings present in the gospel and Christianity finds its mystery only in the living God. Is God indeed the focus of our life? That is also the urgent question for us today, from the perspective of the Matthaean account of Jesus' three temptations.

15

Epiphany: God, but in authentic humanity

(Matthew 2.1-2)

At the word of welcome

Today we really celebrate Christmas for a second time; this time, however, in the style of the Eastern church, where other accents can be heard and Christmas is called the day of the manifestation of God. It is not so much about the little child Jesus as about God's glory which reveals itself in a royal child. That is the theme.

Reading from the Gospel according to Matthew

'Now when Jesus was born in Bethlehem of Judaea in the days of Herod the king, behold, wise men from the East came to Jerusalem, saying, "Where is he who has been born king of the Jews? For we have seen his star in the East, and have come to worship him." When Herod the king heard this, he was troubled, and all Jerusalem with him; and assembling all the chief priests and scribes of the people, he inquired of them where the Christ was to be born. They told him, "In Bethlehem of Judaea; for so it is written by the prophet: 'And you, O Bethlehem, in the land of Judah, are by no means least among the rulers of Judah; for from you shall come a ruler who will govern my people Israel.'" Then Herod summoned the wise men secretly and ascertained from them what time the star appeared; and he sent them to Bethlehem, saying, "Go and search diligently for the child, and when you have found him bring me word, that I too may come and worship him." When they had heard the king they went their way; and lo the star which they had seen in the East went before them, till it came to rest over the place where the child was. When they saw the star, they rejoiced exceedingly with great joy; and going into the house they saw the child with Mary his mother, and they fell down and worshipped him. Then, opening their treasures, they offered him gifts, gold and frankincense and myrrh. And being warned in a dream not to return to Herod, they departed to their own country by another way.'

Homily

We are inclined to raise the question whether at the birth of Jesus a number of magi – wise men or astrologers – did in fact come from the East to worship him as divine. For that is what Matthew's text suggests. The wise men say literally to Herod: 'We have come to prostrate ourselves in homage to him.' We often act as though if this was not an authentic historical event, then the whole story would be meaningless, without religious content. However, legends are sometimes the metaphysic of reality; you must be able to produce all kinds of legends around your own personality! Such stories provide a better sketch of what Jesus was concerned with than some detached, authentically historical facts do.

In order to understand the religious significance of this story we must first survey some of the background.

I. In antiquity it was part of the cultural heritage of the Near East for people to think that every person had his or her own star (among Christians this later was to become a personal 'guardian angel'). It was thought that this star rose at a person's birth and disappeared again at his or her death. For special individuals, those whose lives had been very important for others in one way or another, it seemed (as people told the story subsequently) that something special had also happened at the birth. The birth of such an important person was often associated with the appearance of a particularly striking star, as a herald. Thus ancient stories told of the star of Abraham or the star of Jacob; in the second Jewish War, in 130-135 CE, the great Zealot messianic leader Rabbi Bar Kosiba even altered his name to Bar Kochba, i.e. son of the star. There is also mention in Revelation 12.1 of 'a great sign in heaven' as herald of great things. And we know the expression 'being born under a good star'. Horoscopes have still not disappeared!

Thus being born under a particular star points to the appearance on earth of a very important person, someone who is of great significance for others. Matthew is concerned with such an experience and not with a supernova or Halley's comet to be given an astrological context, as some people think they can claim, in a Babel-like confusion of biblical and astronomical language. It is possible that after the death of Jesus, when Christians had long believed in his resurrection, his birth was connected with an astral phenomenon in the year 9 or 6 BCE reconstructed by scholars, especially a particular constellation of Jupiter, the royal star, and Saturn, the sabbath or Jewish star, which because of their position could be seen at that time as one extra-large star; at least it cannot be ruled out. But this does not add anything to the story in Matthew and he is not at all interested in it. The connection between particular heavenly phenomena and the birth, indeed the life, of an important person was already a well known pattern then. To talk about an important person is to talk about his birth star, whatever this may have been. So even now many people still draw up their own horoscopes. Why might Matthew not be talking in this way? (But it tells us nothing about the possible date of Jesus' birth.)

It is also striking that of the only two evangelists to tell us anything about the birth of Jesus, Matthew in particular describes a visit of wise men from the East who, led by a star, find the house where Jesus is born and bring presents to the newborn Saviour, while Luke knows nothing about it from the start and instead has a story about the visit of shepherds to the manger of which Matthew in turn knows nothing. Moreover neither the Gospel of Mark nor that of John knows anything at all about events around the birth of Jesus. So it is not a question of whether Matthew and Luke want to relate historical facts but of how we must deal with stories in scripture which historically seem improbable, to say the least. What message does Matthew (in contrast to Luke) want to give us with this story, which only in the Middle Ages became the story of the 'three kings'? For Matthew speaks neither of 'three' nor of three 'kings' and certainly not of a Caspar, a beardless young boy; Melchior, a bearded greyhead; and Balthasar, the dark royal type, who later in our crib becomes a black king. All that can happen within our popular Catholic devotion, but here we must not forget the real message of Matthew.

II. As Matthew tells it, the story clearly came into being in a Christian community which had a tense relationship with its Jewish environment. And this also provides the key to the understanding of this Matthaean biblical legend. In the story, Herod, the 'false and bad king of the Jews', is compared with the Christ child, 'the authentic and good king of the Jews'. The first king seeks the life of the second, coming king. Herod was anything but popular in Jerusalem. He was known to be constantly afraid of possible usurpers, real and imaginary, seeking to depose him from the throne. The historian Flavius Josephus himself tells us about one of Herod's plans: anxious that he might lose his throne, he planned a murder of all the newborn children in Judah. Jews had heard of this and the rumour went the rounds. Matthew's story of what was thought to be the real massacre of all Jewish boys under two years of age at the birth of Jesus fits into this. Herod was evidently capable of killing children out of fear. So the people of Jerusalem hated Herod. But at a first reading it is surprising that we hear Matthew say that when people heard of the birth of 'a new king of the Jews', not only Herod but also 'all Jerusalem with him was terrified and confused'. This is news that one would expect to cause joy and popular rejoicing. Matthew evidently looks back on that event from quite a different standpoint. In Matthew the inhabitants of Jerualem are also against Jesus. That indicates a situation of about fifty years after Jesus' death, in which Jews and Christians were living on a very tense footing with one another. Matthew is thinking of the rejection of Jesus by his Jewish fellow-countrymen – historically above all the pro-Roman Sadducees. For Matthew, Jerusalem is the city of the murder of Jesus, the city where the people had cried out, 'His blood be on us and on our children' (Matt.27.25). All this opened the door to the Gentiles in the church of Christ. That too is the focus of this story: the magi are the firstfruits of the Gentiles; this is a prelude to the influx of Gentiles to the messiah of Israel who, while expected by the Jews, came in a way which the Jews had not expected, and the story is therefore at the same time a prelude to the rejection of Jesus by Jerusalem. Therefore Matthew says that at the birth of Jesus 'Herod was afraid and all Jerusalem with him'.

The birth of Jesus, the first Christmas festival, is here clearly understood as a threat to the Jewish establishment, Jerusalem, and to the monarchy: a threat to all who exercise power over their fellow human beings, at least in contrast to God's authority, which is a rule that liberates human beings for freedom. 'The manifestation of the goodness and loving-kindness of God', as the letter to Titus puts it later (Titus 3.4), becomes the beginning of an event which people expect will turn our history on its head and will overthrow established conditions that hurt men and women. It is as if everything that has gained power in a human way unerringly feels the threat from the defenceless Jesus: 'All Jerusalem was afraid!' Such a Jesus discloses people to themselves and unmasks their own consciences, so that they either oppose Jesus and seek his life or repent and fall before him in worship. Matthew wants to make it clear that foreigners accepted Jesus and worshipped him and that his own people, his former fellow-believers, refused to worship him. He arrives at what for us is a somewhat fierce black-and-white contrast because his own Jewish-Christian community evidently had to suffer a good deal from non-Christian Jews.

III. In fact today's festival is the Christmas festival of the Eastern Christian churches. In the Eastern Christmas the emphasis is not so much, as in our Western Christmas, on the child Jesus: the defencelessness and weakness of a helpless baby in the crib (a story that of course we find only in Luke). In the Eastern celebration of Christmas the accent lies on the christological background of the whole event, just as the Matthaean story presents it. It is not for nothing that for the homage paid to the child by the wise men Matthew uses the word *proskynesis*: falling down and prostrating oneself, as one did before Eastern kings, who at that time were revered as sons of the Almighty God. Today's feast is an *epiphany*, a revelation of God in the *royal child* Jesus. That he is a defenceless child disappears as it were in glory behind the religious *frisson* in the face of the divine which is revealed here.

I believe that only the double celebration of Christmas – the Western festival along with the Eastern – can disclose to us all the dimensions of what we may commemorate on these Christmas days. At a separate, special celebration, without the counterpart of the other Christmas festival, we run the danger that the balance may tip one-sidedly *either* towards sentimental romanticism round a baby in a crib, surrounded by the fragrance and the lights of fir trees: childlike defencelessness without divine power which brings salvation, *or* an alien, Eastern monophysite sacral sphere in which, because of a predominance of the divine, defenceless beings begin to suffer from a loss of humanity, suffer from a lack of human blood. Therefore every year we celebrate Christmas so to speak twice: that keeps Christian faith in balance.

16

An ambiguous 'Hosanna': Luke's Palm Sunday

(Luke 19.28-40)

At the word of welcome (Introduction to Holy Week)

Today Holy Week begins. You can look in very different ways at the last days in the life of Jesus, which we begin to commemorate this week. This year, this week is illuminated by the Gospel according to Luke. Above all in connection with the story of the passion of Jesus this Gospel has some peculiarities which we do not find in other Gospels. Here I want to point to just two aspects. For Luke, Holy Week is the last part of Jesus' career, of his missionary journey from Galilee to Jerusalem. Already in 9.51, after Jesus's first two forecasts of his passion, we read literally: 'When the days drew near for him to be received up, he set his face to go to Jerusalem.' Setting one's face towards something means going there deliberately and with firm purpose. For Luke, something essential in Jesus' life is to be accomplished in Jerusalem. It is a kind of exodus, with an entry into Jerusalem imagined as being on a large scale, as a prelude to the dramatic event which is what is of real importance.

In Luke's view, the main agent in all this is not so much the Jews, still less the Romans, but Satan – as the personification of evil. It is Satan who wants to make himself the master of Jesus' disciples. 'Now Satan entered into Judas called Iscariot, who was of the number of the Twelve' (Luke 22.3). Luke lays stress on the fact that the evil which happens here is 'satanic'. People are sometimes so deeply infatuated that they become real devils, really evil, capable of demonic evil. What we hear about tyrants like Duvalier and Marcos who, without blinking an eyelid, but convinced that they were quite right, built up their luxury and prestige at the expense of the suffering of millions of people, in fact flies in the face of all human imagination; it is really as if there was a satanic brain behind them. However, if one believes in human beings, one is also forced to believe in the demonic in our human history. We should really say with a lump in our throats that in Luke's view it was not a Jew, not a Roman, but a follower of Jesus, and thus in a sense an aspiring Christian, who 'betrayed' Jesus. We, Christians, may not forget this during this Holy Week, after all that the last months have recalled of the holocaust, the reality filmed in *Shoah*. That is what the vision of Luke's Gospel also challenges us to do.

Here we should also recall that Luke was writing for Christians from the peoples outside Israel, about ten years after the Jewish War. The proclamation of the 'kingdom of God' and of 'the name of Jesus Christ' had to be brought to life again in those days. Luke wants to make it clear that (in contrast to all kinds of fashionable slogans of that time) it is only from the concrete historical life of Jesus that the great Christian confession of Jesus' redemptive death, sealed by his resurrection, takes on truly human significance.

Homily

By the Roman road from Jericho to Jerusalem one finally came out up on the east flank of the Mount of Olives, from where the descent into the Kidron valley begins, with Jerusalem in sight. According to the sources of this story Jesus had gone with some pilgrims to Jerusalem for a passover feast. Arriving up on the Mount of Olives they see the city of David, Jerusalem, below them, and above all its great temple gleaming in the sun. Despite the threatening Roman citadel of the Antonia, which they also see, at the sight of Jerusalem the pilgrims spontaneously burst into cries of joy, with the traditional greeting from a psalm: 'Blessed is he who comes in the name of the Lord' (Ps.118.26). From Zion comes Israel's 'king of peace' (Zech.9.9). But in Luke's story, written on the basis of belief in Jesus' resurrection, Jesus himself is celebrated as the messianic king of peace. Like other Jews, Jesus comes with a group as a pilgrim to Jerusalem, but in this story, as the pilgrims see the city there below them, he himself is acclaimed as 'the coming one', who has his expectations: the fulfilment of Malachi (3.1; also of Zech.9.9; 14.4-5; Isa.40.9). For Luke, however, he is a coming king. Hence a 'Hosanna!', 'Glory to God in the highest!'

Luke had also said that already in another place, namely at Jesus' birth: 'Glory to God in the highest and on earth peace among men...' (Luke 2.14). Now, however, he does not say precisely the same thing. The 'Gloria in excelsis' of Christmas Day is ambiguous. Now Luke says: 'Blessed is the king who comes in the name of the Lord. Peace *in heaven* and glory in the highest' (Luke 19.38). There is peace in heaven, but evidently not yet on earth: there is no longer any mention of 'peace on earth'. That is no coincidence. Jesus' entry into Jerusalem is not yet the coming of messianic peace on earth. In his story Luke wants to explain what 'messiah' and 'king of peace' really mean. It is not at all what people expect. Only Jesus' specific way of life can explain to us what these highly eminent titles, well known at the time, really mean: the one acclaimed messianic king will be condemned to crucifixion before the week is out. *If* Jesus is messiah, *if* he is king, Lord, indeed Son of God, then he is so only *as the one condemned to crucifixion by human beings* (see Luke 24.26). Here power and prestige can be seen only in disarming weakness and humiliation. And if that is so, these titles which denote great lords, VIPs and wise men must first be thoroughly purged of all the dimensions of power which they suggest. 'He judged the cause of the poor and needy; then it was well. Is this not to know me? says the Lord' (Jer.22.16). Had that not already been said by a former prophet? Jesus, who had come blessing and healing, opening up communication from Palestine to Jerusalem, would within a few days bleed to death outside the gates of Jerusalem on a Roman cross.

Christ is not a myth but a living person who (according to the Greek version of the creed) '*was crucified under Pontius Pilate*'. That is not there for nothing. Tyrannical power exterminated Jesus in a corner of the world; powerful men did away with him. This creed seeks to be a constant reminder of this, just as nowadays the 'crazy mothers' in Argentina remain with us as a constant reminder of their vanished children. Without that cross of the historical man Jesus of Nazareth, 'the Christ' of our Christian churches is purely a myth; perhaps an idea which is a strong motive force that becomes historically effective, but in fact then only in the service of the powerful: a messiah on a charger, not God's anointed on an ass. Only a constant falling back on Jesus' concrete, historical career can avoid the abstract domination of confessional titles of honour, demoting the vulnerable man Jesus to an outmoded religious or cultural myth. The Jesus of history therefore gets all the emphasis in the Gospel of Luke. The historical reality of Jesus continues to resist all attempts, even by the church, to annex him or fix him in a dominant 'Christ image' which is not subject to the norm of the 'living person' of our history, Jesus of Nazareth.

Within the context of our own lives and on the basis of the historical fact of Jesus' career, message and way of life, we need time and again to explain the meaning of the Hosanna on Palm Sunday. For according to Luke Palm Sunday also contains a criticism of the alleluia of confessing churches which is sometimes misused, a hosanna that is often set against the personal and political commitment in the *praxis* of Christians in favour of 'the least among us': the *little ones.* At the end of this celebration we shall hear again from Luke the negative contrast to this festal story, for in Luke an early Christian recollection of Jesus' weeping over the city of Jerusalem is deliberately put immediately after the story of the Hosanna on Palm Sunday.

17

'My ways are not your ways'

(Isaiah 55.8)

A Good Friday meditation

'Thus says the Lord: My ways are not your ways.' By contrast, we are too concerned to have our own way, to mark it out ourselves very carefully against what others want; there is something of the territorial imperative in us human beings. We even want to set the direction of our spiritual lives ourselves. But in that case we are often brought up against a brick wall and in the end we begin to torment ourselves either with questions about the constant failure of others to understand us or with accusations against ourselves like: 'I'm a failure; things never succeed for me and something is always going wrong.' Here I often think of a number of Old Testament texts in which as many as three times it is said that someone, usually a patriarch, on dying blesses his two sons, but *cancellatis manibus*, as the Vulgate aptly says, i.e. with crossed arms, so that the main and most powerful blessing (that of the right hand) did not fall on the head of the oldest son who sat at his father's right hand (as was his due), but on the youngest, who sat on the left (see e.g. Gen.48.9-20). God plays with the right of the firstborn to his heritage; God turns all human expectations and calculations upside down. Even Jesus only gradually became aware that the coming of the kingdom of God would not take place during his lifetime (as he certainly thought originally) but that he would be removed from this world by a violent death like John the Baptist, his first inspiration and teacher. So Jesus could happily pray to the Father that his kingdom might come through us human beings hallowing his name by doing his will, on earth, here and now, as the angels had long done it in heaven. He then prayed that his and our Father would indeed exercise the threefold function of a Jewish father: namely to provide for the daily needs of his children; forgive them the wrong they had done if they truly regretted it; and finally protect them against all evil. The Jesus who prayed like this experienced on the cross that even his prayer was more of a solitary monologue than a dialogue with word and response. Those who authentically seek personal contact with God get the impression in their prayers of only hearing the empty echo of their own voices.

Years ago I was standing in Brussels waiting for a bus to take me to Louvain. A young man was standing a few yards away by a lamp-post; he was extremely nervous. He was evidently waiting for a girl and I thought that the time for their date must long be past. He began to stamp his feet with impatience, and seemed start talking to himself, to the point that I heard him say, 'Mais chérie, viens donc,' 'Come on, darling', though there was no sign of any beloved. In expectation of a personal encounter he had begun to talk to the girl who was coming. Now is this a monologue or a dialogue? I think that it is a dialogue. And it is the same with our prayers and with the prayer of Jesus on the cross: 'My God, my God, why hast thou forsaken me?'

The desperate attempts that we human beings often display in making ourselves irreplaceable again reflects how things in fact are in our world, namely that within the game that our society plays, every human being is a disposable article. People are assessed by their prestige and success, honoured for both and then pushed to one side, the flotsam of our history. But I would assert that Jesus' experience, though never grim, was just as little a permanent alleluia mood. The Gospels of Mark and Matthew relate that Jesus died 'with a loud cry' (Mark 15.37; Matt.27.50), a shriek. The day before yesterday, in a discussion group which meets every two weeks, a colleague who had made a journey to the poorest people of Chile said that he had no words for describing the situation there: seventy per cent of the poor had no income at all! And that is only one bit of our great world. Against the background of a history of suffering and injustice and with a career of Jesus who in love identified himself with the suffering and injustice of others so radically that for that very reason he was swept out of our society's game, the word *God* can hardly be spoken other than in a loud cry of grief and dismay, of disquiet and indignation, and at the same time of almost unspoken but reckless hope for reconciliation. Is it not in following the actions of Jesus, of which his message was an intrinsic element, that the most sensitive place is to be found, where what we indicate with a great word, namely *religious experience*, becomes possible and fruitful?

Some scholars have thought that Jesus' suffering and death was brought about by a tragic misunderstanding on the part of both the Jewish authorities and the Romans. But that makes what Jesus proclaimed and did irrelevant, indeed insignificant. In that way the radicalism of Jesus' message, backed up by his consistent action, is neutralized, and then the door is opened for a sheer alleluia Christianity, an Easter without Good Friday! Where Jesus' radicalism, which consisted in his identification with the suffering of others out of concern for them, knows no boundaries, 'this evil world' is fatally struck by a love which makes itself vulnerable; but for that reason this world, too, embarks on an equally radical opposition to the threat-from-love, and the one who proclaims and shows love is seen by the powers as a threat... and thus liquidated. So let us keep our Alleluia for Easter Day and only then let us strike up tones of joy. But let us do it then.

I would want to call Jesus' sacrifice on the cross 'the vain offering of love'; just as Mary Magdalene broke the jar and anointed Jesus' feet with the precious ointment in vain generosity, in an uncalculating spilling (which the calculating Judas found very hard to take). That is how Jesus spilt his life in vain for men and women! 'In vain', but not idly and emptily. In vain, because people are still tortured and crucified in one way or another. That cross did not in fact need to have to been... just as God did not need it: God is not to be reduced to *a function of* human beings, of the world or of society. God is a useless, superfluous hypothesis for all this. We also see that many people can lead meaningful lives without believing in God. That is possible. God is there as 'pure gratuitousness', even pure freedom; brand new every day; without a reason why. It is like when someone gives us a bunch of flowers and we say, 'You didn't need to do that.' But not needing to do it is the supreme luxury of our human life; and in the same way God too is the luxury of our life. Our luxury, not so much our cause or our goal. He is pure, excessive luxury! Therefore we too are called to a love which dares 'vainly'. If the basic symbol of God is living humankind, then the place where human beings are dishonoured, insulted and tortured becomes, both in the depth of our own hearts and in the society which oppresses men and women, at the same time the privileged place where (above all in our time) *religious experience*, indeed mysticism, becomes possible, precisely *in* a way of life and human action that seeks to give shape to this symbol and heal, and wants to raise it up and bring it to itself: home to his or her deepest truth. And only then is religious experience also possible wherever human beings find it also in the depths with one another, or even enjoy it in nature.

In the action of Jesus, extending to the helplessness of his complete, vulnerable love on the cross, we may hear God's confirmation, 'Yes, you may *live*.'

18

The Johannine Easter: The feast of the giving of the Spirit

'Do not quench the Spirit' (I Thess 5.19)

(John 20.19-23)

At the word of welcome

For many years people have complained in spiritual literature that 'the Holy Spirit' is neglected in the Western church. People have said and still say that the Spirit remains the great unknown, indeed the forgotten one. This complaint can be read in all the books that have appeared about the Holy Spirit in recent years, evidently with the tacit promise that this or that new book will change the situation. But after reading these books you note that they don't get you any further. Does this not suggest that the Spirit of God *is* perhaps indeed the great unknown and *wills to remain* so, like the wind that you do not see but which moves everything, keeps it alive and makes it vibrate? Perhaps we have to look for another way of catching the Holy Spirit in the act.

Homily

We will do better to investigate, i.e. to learn to see and hear, what the fruits of the Spirit are than directly to ask after his name and credentials. The Acts of the Apostles give us this advice indirectly. In Peter's so-called Pentecost sermon it is said: 'Being therefore exalted at the right hand of God, and having received from the Father the promise of the Holy Spirit, he has poured out this *which you see and hear*' (Acts 2.33). The Spirit is something or someone that you must seek in its effects. If that is the case, we cannot avoid beginning with the story of a person of whom it is told that, when he was about thirty years old, he began to travel round his native region 'in the power of the Spirit'. In Nazareth, where he had grown up, one sabbath he reads out in the synagogue a passage from the prophet Isaiah: 'The Spirit of the Lord is upon me, because he has anointed me to preach good news to the poor. He has sent me to proclaim release to the captives and recovering of sight to the blind, to set at liberty those who are oppressed...' And he closed the book, sat down and said, 'Today this scripture has been fulfilled in your hearing' (Luke 4.16-21). That is how it begins. This Spirit of the beginning, which blew over the coming creation as the breath of God, this stormy wind, this unknown force, seems to have taken possession of someone who in a few words unfolds a vision of liberation for men and women who are alienated from themselves and from their brothers and sisters. We hear: 'You are restored to yourself: thanks to the Spirit you may finally be human.'

The story then tells how Jesus himself lives out that vision and how some individuals follow him in doing so. He perishes in the attempt, and on the day of his death all, apart from a few women, leave him in the lurch. But despite this death the vision seems to live on, above all thanks to these women. A community comes into being from the power of this same Spirit: 'They were of one heart and soul, and no one said that any of the things which he possessed was his own, but they had everything in common; a great power went out for them; for there was not a needy person among them' (Acts 4.32). That is what we read.

Did that really happen, or was it all wishful thinking?

Will there ever be a time when people are so full of Holy Spirit that they are capable of living in freedom for one another, that the least become the most precious, that love is a light burden and community a reality that exceeds all dreams? That they are full of the Holy Spirit and forgive one another's sins and rudenesses? 'Today these words are fulfilled', says Jesus. That applies to our Pentecost today, 22 May 1988. But in that case, *even now* people must arise among us and band together to hold the vision high and hand it on. Believing in the Holy Spirit means that we are still infected by the same words: to bring good news to the poor, to cry liberation to the captives and to make the oppressed walk in freedom. Over the centuries and through these centuries there has been a kind of constant which is constantly repeated and puts itself forward and which unites us with countless people before us.

The history of the Spirit, effective in Jesus' life-work, in his death and resurrection and afterwards in his community, the church, has a long history. Already at the beginning of creation the breath of God blew over the primal chaos, and Psalm 104, which reflects on this, says of it: 'When you send forth your breath, they are created; and you renew the face of the ground.' But we recall above all the powerful vision of Ezekiel 37: the southern kingdom, Judah, is dead. The bones of the inhabitants lie drying up in a valley. The Spirit of God brings the prophet to this valley and he has to proclaim there: 'I shall bring the spirit of life into you and you shall come alive again.' The Spirit blows over the bones and indeed they live. Spirit brings life, drives away chaos, corruption and death.

That is the Jewish story. The Christians picked up the thread of this story and the story acquired a sequel. We do not come into this chapel for a performance, a reading or a sermon, for what this or that man or woman has to tell us. We come here because we want to hold firm to one another *in this Spirit*. Because the vision by which we want to live must be shared and borne together, if it is to remain a productive vision. Otherwise the Spirit is quenched. We are here because we form an affinity of spirit with one another, because from moment to moment and week to week we want to work for more justice for more people. Justice, overflowing in love. For it is *for that* that the Spirit rests on us, according to Isaiah and Jesus' biblical sermon, that sabbath in Nazareth.

Paul says that the Spirit reveals himself in each of us: each has his own gifts with which to be of service to all (I Cor.12). In all these different people the Spirit evokes the vision of the coming world. If there has to be boasting – though this is of no use, says Paul (II Cor.12.1) – then it is for that sort of people. Those who do not give up. Those who are restless. Those who burn out and do not find that amiss. Those who sometimes overtax themselves and cannot nor would not do otherwise. Paul calls them 'fools', for of course they are nothing. They cannot do much. It is the power of the Spirit in them which achieves something.

In ancient writings and liturgical texts Christians have tried to give the Spirit a name, many names: not abstract titles but words of flesh and blood. Wind, breath of life, comforter, helper, father of the poor, the one who dries tears, the feminine face of God. Spirit is a heartfelt desire, a passion: spiritual passion. A mediaeval mystic calls it 'the mystical laugh'; he is the Spirit, the pushing power, of God, a squall and breath of life. Sometimes the pictures suddenly change: 'spirit' then becomes an unquenchable fire, warmth, fiery tongues; spiritual anointing; a power which prompts people to unheard-of deeds, getting them going, keeping them going. making space in chaos. It is a Spirit which breaks with the law, with a letter that kills; a spirit of space which God gives to men and women in Jesus. We can speak of the Spirit only in images, in many languages and tongues. Spirit brings repose to the startled, warms those who are petrified with cold and heals those who are wounded. And new liturgical songs describe the Spirit in the same way: 'The Spirit of God is like a fire, like fierce flames, consuming any injustice, a glow of compassion... The Spirit of God works in the stillness, drives on with gentle power, a wise mother who holds us, a source of good powers. It gives us courage to endure, helps people to understand one another again, surrounds us like a cloak' (M.Koyck). Finally the Spirit is God's '*cri de coeur*'. 'Spirit of God' is an incalculable, astonishing risk taken by God!

How can I sum up this enthralling process? *God's Spirit is a spirit 'which makes all things new'*. Human history is full of stories about such spots: a spot where it is good for people to dwell; where nothing is wanting, where you can do as you will: this is sometimes called Ithaca, or Arcadia, Never-Never Land, Utopia, the Promised Land; scripture says that it is a land where there will be no more tears, no abyss, no death and no curse. The Book of Revelation (20.11-21.5) says that it is a city with ever-open doors, a city of crystal that you can see through, sparkling, unbreakable. 'And the streets of the city were of pure gold, transparent as glass.' That means that we, people of the future, people filled with the Spirit, will become transparent, shot through with light; all that is dark in us, our past, our inhibitions, our mistakes and blockages – whatever remains hidden, all the blockages in us which make us dumb to one another – all this 'oldness' is then past. There will be no more night. All is new.

Pentecost is not really a feast *in honour of the Holy Spirit*, a so-called 'third God' in a divine three-member family. The Spirit is and remains the real redemptive gift of Jesus as the Christ, 'the man of God': 'the Father and I are one.' Pentecost is a feast of Christ. Pentecost has to do with the Jew Jesus of Nazareth. The Fourth Gospel tells us that when Jesus was still on earth, 'Spirit' was not yet; the reason for this is 'because this Nazarene was not yet glorified' (John 7.39). Elsewhere in the Gospel we read: 'It is to your advantage that I go away, for if I do not go away, the Counsellor will not come to you; but if I go, I will send him to you' (John 17.7).

The exegete Fr Lagrange once wrote that he could not at all understand the significance of that connection between the earthly Jesus, who cannot give the Spirit, and the risen Christ who can; in the end he gave up looking for a solution and said, 'C'est le sécret de Dieu': this relationship is the mystery of God; human beings understand nothing of it.

However, we may not forget that according to all the Gospels the Spirit is the real redemptive gift of the risen, glorified Jesus. The Gospel of John does not set the scene of the gift of the Spirit on the fiftieth day after Easter, like Luke and all Christian liturgy, but on Easter Day itself: the Spirit is the Easter gift of Jesus the Christ. In the oldest texts of Paul the glorified Jesus is himself called 'pneuma', spirit (II Cor.3.17), because he is taken up into the life of God's own world. The Fourth Gospel says that only then can he send the Spirit, *from the Father*. For this Gospel, Spirit does not come from this world but from above: 'Spirit' can only be given 'from the Father'.

Redemption is something from God, a gift of God, not a human work. But through the gift of the Spirit the redemption and liberation becomes the work of spirit-filled people – of Jesus and all who follow him, in his spirit.

'Spirit', the passion of the Spirit (enthusiasm) and the power of the Spirit, cannot therefore be bought; you cannot make any payment, as a certain Simon thought when he offered the apostles money in order to be able to receive the laying on of hands through which the Holy Spirit is given (Acts 8.18-24). Thereupon Peter exclaims, as it were: 'To hell with your money if you think that you can buy God's gift with it.' Pentecost, as a feast of the gift of the Spirit to the community of faith and all individual believers, is in fact the feast of the incalculable and unexpected gift: in ancient hymns, moreover, the Spirit is also called *donum Dei*, a gift of God. And another ancient hymn calls it both 'giver' and 'gift'. 'Spirit of God' points to the heavenly or the divine power in all Christian life: Christian life is pure divine gift, the grace-filled passion of the Spirit – not an achievement.

Paul heaps up the intensifying prefixes in a Greek word (*syn-anti-lambanesthai*) in order to express how the Spirit 'fixes itself extremely firmly' to us in order to help us, seizes hold of our weakness in order to allow the power of God to come to fruition in our weakness and to renew us from within (Rom.8.26): 'Likewise the Spirit helps us in our weakness; for we do not know how to pray as we ought. But the Spirit himself intercedes with us with sighs too deep for words... The Spirit intercedes for the saints according to the will of God' (Rom.8.16-17). Anyone who in practice believes in Jesus the Christ now already, but above all at the last judgment, has the Holy Spirit alongside as advocate. Such a person does not need to have any anxiety. This advocate, the Spirit, can write straight on crooked human lines.

However, I cannot end this homily without saying a word about what in various places in the New Testament is called the *unforgivable sin against the Holy Spirit*. This tradition is present in too many New Testament passages which are independent of one another for us to be able to get round it diplomatically or argue it away. I find the most pointed expression of this tradition in the Letter to the Hebrews. There it is both matter-of-fact and dramatic at the same time: 'For it is impossible to restore again to repentance those who have once been enlightened, who have tasted the heavenly gift, and have become partakers of the Holy Spirit, and have tasted the goodness of the word of God and the powers of the age to come, if they then commit apostasy, since they crucify the Son of God on their own account' (Heb.4.4-6). This passage, which is perhaps crude to human ears and in any case is dramatic, says more about the inexpressible luxury of the experience of the Holy Spirit and the foretaste given there of the new heaven and the new earth which is brought about by it than about the possibility that people should turn their backs on such an intense experience and repudiate it.

Pentecost today, that is the celebration of Jesus of Nazareth as the Christ, i.e. as the Messiah who sends us his messianic gift, the Spirit. On this day we celebrate forgiveness of sins. It is a festival in which people forgive one another what they have done to one another and do to one another every day. It is a festival of being concerned for our fellow human beings through the *passion of the Spirit.* It is a festival of tenderness and making tender, because – often unconsciously – we unnecessarily cause one another a good deal of sorrow.

19

Sharing bread: Sacrament Day or 'Corpus Christi'

'Corpus Christi' as community of solidarity and liberation
(Mark 14.12-16, 22-26)

At the word of welcome

The words 'Sacrament Day' remind us that believers in fact deal with reality in two different ways which influence each other. On the one hand there is everyday reality, 'worldly reality'. On the other hand we can also experience the same reality sacramentally and elevate it to a symbolic but nevertheless real level of reality. There is everyday worldly reality in which people are often like wolves preying on one another, grabbing and scavenging: a world of injustice and oppression, in short a history of disaster and suffering. Many good things also happen in this worldly world, but we will never be certain whether good or evil will have the last word in it. To give form to the certainty of faith that good and not evil will have the last word, we need the sacramental world. That is the context into which I want to put the celebration of today's liturgy.

Homily

I said that believers deal with reality in two different ways. How does that work out in practice?

On the one hand there are laden tables. Elsewhere, empty tables, no bread, no rice. At this level of everyday worldly reality, breaking bread literally means seeing that everyone has something to eat: we must share the bread and live and organize our society in such a way that there is bread for everyone. But prophets who challenge the injustice and the heart-rending inequality of opportunity in this-worldly reality are done away with by the existing order as spoil-sports. Yet these spoil-sports open up the possibility of another, better and even definitively good future opened up by God in Jesus of Nazareth. The transformation of the history of disaster and suffering into a history of salvation and brotherly and sisterly solidarity is mediated through the sacramental world of 'corpus Christi', the eucharist. I want to explore this.

Alongside the worldly breaking and sharing of bread there is also the *sacramental* reality of breaking bread. At this level of reality, through visible and emotionally laden language and signs we grope for the invisible future which is not yet realized. In the liturgy our eyes begin to open. We see in the symbolic breaking of the bread the reality of a life that goes through into the future, to God, where there is bread for everyone. The life of Jesus which was violently broken off on the cross, his silenced message, his option for unrealized justice, are taken up into the invisible reality of God who gives us a sign or sacrament of this coming reality: *Jesus lives*.

Bishop Romero was able to say some weeks before he was murdered: 'They can kill me, but not the voice of justice.' It was possible for this saying to be true only because of Jesus the Risen One. Without the Risen One the voice of justice would indeed continue to resound because people still refuse to treat evil on an equal footing with good. But without the Risen One we should not know whether this voice will ever be heard or will be smothered at every turn. For to commemorate the dead Jesus in the eucharist is not to trumpet around that Jesus was killed because he became the dupe of the superior power of earthly forces. This death of Jesus is taken up into a 'sacramental world'; the sacramental proclamation of the death of Jesus is the celebration of the Living One. Without the resurrection of Jesus his death was in vain, just as (without this resurrection) the death of Martin Luther King, Bishop Romero and so many others clearly show that in our history the evil powers of this world are often the victors. But in the eucharistic celebration of the dead but risen Jesus we confess something else. There we celebrate in the order of sacramental reality the fact that what on the level of actual daily life is the superior power of earthly forces is ultimately the disarming of them. Therefore we now set down already, in our earthly history, here and there, signs and traces of a coming new world.

The memory of Jesus' death led his followers to challenge these powers now already in our history and to banish meaningless death. What from a historical perspective, in the eyes of worldly reality, means the end of a dream, Jesus' crucifixion, by virtue of sacramental reality becomes an effective utopia in our history: the promise on the basis of which the worldly powers are disarmed. To break bread sacramentally also signifies that even death is no enemy. For although the powers threaten torture and death, there is no longer a sting to this threat since Jesus rose from the dead and sat at table with his friends. God is a God of life, even in circumstances in which we experience more death than life.

Our sharing of bread is not in vain

But all this does not mean that we let the earthly reality of *homo homini lupus*, the history of human beings being wolves to one another, run its course and then naively and innocently continue to break bread with one another, as though nothing were the matter! Precisely through the eucharist we are challenged at the level of our history to realize as much as possible of what we celebrate sacramentally: bread for all, salvation and liberation for all. The eucharistic Christ is really present as bread for the poor. The Christ who is sacramentally present stands surety that our sharing of the bread, too, is not in vain. In order to see through worldly reality in its deepest injustice we need the wider view of the sacrament, the 'Corpus Christi' as brotherly and sisterly solidarity, church community with Jesus as the head of this body. And in order to keep this eucharistic reality credible, we have to devote ourselves to a better, juster world. Without the resurrection of Jesus our faith is pure superstructure suspended in the air. But on the other hand faith in Jesus' resurrection can itself be an unproductive or dangerous ideology if it does not stimulate us actually to share bread at the level of social policy and in the dimension of our earthly history.

Celebrating the eucharist we confess that the everyday history of injustice and inequality does not have the last word. In the liturgy we confess that in the end the powerful do not have the last word. We may not trivialize the barren, barbarian everyday reality of injustice, poverty and world hunger when we celebrate the eucharist on Sunday in a happy and relaxed way. Nevertheless, in the liturgy we move away from everyday life, and we dwell in a world in which we confess our faith and celebrate our hope. We dwell in the world of the sacramental word and the sacramental sign. We confess and celebrate there the dimension of faith and immense hope for the future. There we celebrate a future which is still not there but which is opened to us through God in Jesus as a future which is also possible for us. *Why him and not us?* However, if we do not collaborate with God's grace, if we do not follow Jesus in actual love and dedication for men and women, then the coming of this better future is sheer ideology.

The dead but risen Jesus is indeed really present in the eucharist. He is ready to be bread above all for the poor, those without bread.

Sacrament Day shows that there is already one who has entered the still untrodden land and indicates to us how we must get there. It is by changing the worldly reality of helplessness and the lust for power, of harshness and anxiety. It is by breaking through our boundaries to the other. He is really present as the living sacramental word; his life and death were not in vain. We for our part proclaim his death until he comes, because in the eucharist we confess that God has put an end to death, destruction and injustice and those who believe in God or at least dedicate themselves to the good of their fellow human beings without reservation can do the same.

Our hope is raised up again

We go to put bread and wine on the table and we hear the words, 'We proclaim the death of the Lord until he comes' (I Cor.11.26). We proclaim the death of *the Lord*, i.e. not his physical death but this death as taken up into the sacramental world of the Risen One among us, the Lord. There is also future for us! In the sacramental celebration of the breaking of the bread we move in a sacramental, utopian world. It is a space where we truly acclaim: this is how God wants the future to be for all men and women, just as we give one another a piece of bread today, so that all shall be satisfied and no one among us shall go away hungry. That is the powerful, stimulating symbolism of this small gesture of breaking a piece of bread. So, after this celebration of the eucharist, when we have returned to so-called 'secular life', each in his or her perhaps small-scale environment, we must dedicate ourselves to a more just, better world for all. At the same time the feast of Corpus Christi intrinsically has something to do with the famine of two-thirds of the world's population, but it is not a gathering in which we look for technical solutions to this problem. It is the sacramental place in which we celebrate the confession of faith in the Risen Jesus who opens up the possibility of a better world. It is the place in which we celebrate that this hope is constantly 'recharged'.

We periodically need this sacramental recharging and re-mobilizing of our hope. Not too much, so that the dynamic of hope does not fade into routine; not too little, so that we do not lose hope. But we need a periodical recharging because worldly reality constantly contradicts what we celebrate here. So we may not reduce the 'worldly' and the 'sacramental' significance of the bread to each other. Far less should we separate them, as though one were purely human and secular and only the other were really Christian. They supplement each other. In the liturgy we are not engaging in social and political action but in a sacramental celebration, a memorial or commemoration: the recollection of Jesus' life and death, in the conviction in faith of his resurrection as Lord, sitting in God's place of honour as the advocate of poor and oppressed people who have no bread.

Whenever we reflect on all this in meditation, Corpus Christi again becomes the feast of brotherly and sisterly 'communion'. *Corpus* as a community of solidarity with all. Thanks to the celebration of the faith that there is bread and life for all, if we ourselves in fact do something about it on the level of everyday life.

That is the message of Sacrament Day.

Intercession

We pray to God,
our merciful Father:

That we may break our bread with others
and share life with one another;

that we may do this
in order to remember him
who asked us to do
what he had done before.

20

God allows himself to be found among the little ones and those of no account

Christ the King in the key minor

(Matthew 25.31-45)

Welcome

In the liturgy, today we celebrate Christ the King, the last Sunday of the year, on the eve of what from a church point of view is 'New Year Sunday'. Here we are completely out of phase with our ordinary human life, for we Christians also in fact celebrate New Year's Eve on December 31 as the ultimate end of one year and the beginning of a new one. Let us listen to what the liturgy today has to tell us and what on the basis of the Gospel of Matthew it calls the 'ultimate end'.

Homily

We had sought God among the great and powerful, but Jesus lets us find God among the little ones and those of no account.

In olden days, and also in the time of Jesus, it was the custom in Palestine to let the sheep and goats graze together during the day under the watchful eye of the shepherd, but before nightfall the shepherd would always divide his flock: the sheep remained outside, while the goats, more sensitive to the cold, went into the fold. Matthew uses this image from the shepherd's world to talk about the judgment on human conduct.

There are three things that we must never forget in reading the Gospel of Matthew. First of all, recently various connections have increasingly been discovered between the tradition of Matthew and the Johannine tradition; that is also the case in this story of Matthew's about the judgment. This helps us to understand this story better: in Matthew, too, the death of Jesus is seen as an exaltation and glorification which makes Jesus judge over all, and the crucifixion itself becomes the criterion by which judgment will be made. Secondly, in this pericope too we must recall Matthew's own view of the kingdom of God, which has much in common with that of Paul.

There is a distinction here between 'the kingdom of heaven', i.e. the kingdom of the Messiah Jesus, and 'the kingdom of God' or the kingdom of the Father, which will only arrive when Jesus has pronounced the final judgment on his own messianic kingdom. Only then will God be all in all. Thirdly, and lastly: this story about a dividing of the peoples by the judge of the world follows two parables with which the story of the judgment on the peoples forms a unit, namely as a third parable about entering the kingdom of heaven; and the passion narrative follows directly after these three parables in Matthew: 'Then the Son of man will be handed over to be crucified' (Matt.26.2). The Son of man who in chapter 25, which was the gospel reading, appears as the glorious judge is ignominiously crucified in the narrative of chapter 26. But in that case the question is whether according to this composition Jesus' death on the cross is not itself the judgment on the world of the nations. And this is clearly the case with Matthew, just as it is in the Gospel of John.

This story about the so-called last judgment is peculiar to Matthew; we do not find any direct parallel to it in the other Gospels. But its background is certainly what the early Christian tradition, expressed in Mark 8.38, says: 'If anyone is ashamed of me and my words... of him shall the Son of Man also be ashamed when he comes in the glory of the Father, surrounded by the holy angels.' But what connects Matthew and John with each other here is the view of Jesus' crucifixion which they both hold: in contrast to Mark, both already see the death as exaltation or glorification of Jesus with the Father.

The story seeks to show that Jesus is great, glorious, kingly precisely in the shameful humiliation of his death on the cross: more clearly than during Jesus' life, in and through his crucifixion it can be seen that Jesus identifies himself with the rejected: with 'the least' among us. That is also the keyword throughout this story. In antiquity, and also in the Old Testament, one could not imagine the lord or king of a kingdom without his being lord and king over his people. Therefore Matthew makes all the peoples appear before the Son of man, who is suddenly called king here: by his death and resurrection Jesus becomes the Lord of the provisional, messianic kingdom. Just as in the John tradition, the Gospel of Matthew also shows that the 'day of God's visitation of his people Israel' coincides with the whole of Jesus' life-work and that the significance of this earthly career of Jesus reaches a climax in the apparent fiasco of his death on the cross, i.e. in his identification with outcast men and women, the dregs of our human history. This identification of Jesus with the poor and the little ones, as this is shown most sharply in his death on the cross, becomes the norm for the last judgment upon us all, upon all peoples. We had sought God among the great and powerful, but Jesus shows that he is only to be found among the little ones and the least: among the black youths who wash the shoes of a white boss for starvation wages; among the many fugitives from tyrannized countries; among the tortured and handicapped, the hungry in Ethiopia and the Sahel; and the multitudes of the marginalized and lonely people in our society.

For Matthew, as for the Gospel of John, Jesus' career, culminating in his death on the cross, is itself the first fundamental judgment on the peoples: it is as it were the first element in the last judgment and has in part already been made, especially in the answer which people have given, whether knowingly or not, to this humiliation of the crucifixion. A first division between the peoples is made by belief or unbelief in Jesus' career to the death, by belief or unbelief in the power of his humiliation as identification with insignificant men and women. But a second and definitive division follows. A part is also played in the judgment by the tension between the 'now already' – the judgment has already been made – and the 'not yet' – the final verdict has still to be passed.

This parable from the Gospel of Matthew is a commentary on Jesus' earthly ministry, suffering and death and a summary of it. Matthew gives pointed expression to this in the first two verses of this story. 'When the Son of Man shall come in his glory, THEN he shall take his place on his throne of glory,' i.e. it is precisely by and in his death (which Matthew now goes on to relate) that Jesus comes in his glory; this death is itself, as in John, already a judgment on all peoples, an anticipation of the last judgment. This death brings about a first dividing of individuals. But there is also a final, definitive dividing. Those who perhaps stood at the left hand at the time of the first dividing (Matt.25.33) can then stand on the right hand if (perhaps not knowing Jesus) they in fact identified themselves with the least, those with whom Jesus had identified himself. Then in his judgment Jesus also identifies himself with them, and only then will the royal Son of man let them enter a completely new kingdom, that of the Father: 'Come, blessed of my Father, and receive the kingdom that is prepared for you from the beginning of the world' (Matt.25.34).

So the heart of the story lies in the opening verse of this parable: 'When the Son of Man comes in his glory', and in Matthew that is not the so-called second coming or coming again of Christ but the greatness which he shows in his humiliating death on the cross: he himself becomes the rejected one. The cross itself becomes the throne and also the norm, the criterion at the judgment. This is what Jesus later says in the Gospel of Matthew before the Sanhedrin: '*From now on* (i.e. from the death sentence and his subsequent death) you shall see the Son of Man sitting at the right hand and coming on the clouds of heaven' (Matt.26.64b). Jesus' crucifixion is his exaltation to the

Father and at the same time a judgment (i.e. he comes on the clouds of heaven to judge, according to the image of the book of Daniel). Through the prism of Jesus' crucifixion as the supreme exaltation in the deepest humiliation, in identification with the least and above all the rejected among us – by himself being rejected – this story offers a perspective on the definitive last judgment of all.

The admonitory instruction that we hear in this parable is clear: a first dividing of the peoples comes about as they give a positive or negative answer to the significance of Jesus' crucifixion as an exaltation in humiliation. Christians have given their affirmative answer to this in faith: they have already passed the first stage of the final judgment successfully. But the second and definitive division can also affect Christians. The criterion of this judgment is the same as in the first dividing: to what degree have Christians expressed their affirmative answer of faith in their actions, especially through the praxis of the kingdom of heaven? Have we identified ourselves with the least among our brethren? Anyone who stood at the right hand in the first dividing may stand on the left at the definitive dividing, and vice versa: the practice of offering a cup of water is decisive. If we are to sense the hard challenge of this judgment we must not just take the Palestinian imagery which Jesus uses literally – giving a glass of water to the thirsty, visiting the prisoners, clothing people chilled to the bone with poverty, and so on – but also give it content for our own time. To the adulterous woman Jesus says, 'Go in peace, but do not do it again.' To people, however, including Christians, who have not welcomed strangers but have insulted them, who have not helped these poor sufferers, who discriminate against their fellow men and women, and so on, this final judge is improbably merciless: 'Depart from me' (Matt.25.41), by your behaviour you have already wished yourself in hell. You yourself did not want to listen to them and you must take the consequences; moreover you do not belong with them – among the lowly ones who have been exalted, whose former tears are now wiped away and forgotten.

The earnestness of this message does not take away its happiness. The ultimate end is in the midst of our daily life; so we too can now, already, celebrate the ultimate end... if we look round at our brothers and sisters, and above all the least among men and women. This is really a very simply gospel message – and a simple way of life.

III · Christians' Problems about God

21

The believer's complaint: 'You are a hidden God'

(Isaiah 45.15)

Dear brothers and sisters

One of the most profound experiences of religious men and women is given sharp expression in the books of the Old Testament. The prophet Isaiah says, 'You are a hidden God' (Isa.45.15), and the book of Kings: 'The Lord said that he would dwell in thick darkness' (I Kings 8.12; II Chron.6.1). The New Testament adds: 'God dwells in light inaccessible' (I Tim.6.16). We ourselves experience this every day. It seems to be a basic law of spiritual life. It is not for nothing that the Gospel of John also says with reference to Jesus: 'It is good for you that I go away.' Absence, going away, seems to be a grace! Seeking God, not so much finding him, is the basic law of the religious life. An eternal but very resolute '*Noli me tangere*' (Don't touch me) has God continually dwelling again in the cloud; even on Ascension Day.

Some time ago I received a letter from a mission sister which included the following words: 'Does belonging to God then consist only in fulfilling his will? It seems to me that I used to see and that now everything is dark, that it is getting darker and more difficult. I no longer have any enthusiasm. I feel utterly alone, as if I belonged to no one. I live in cold faith. Our dear Lord wants us to love him, to please him, yes, but never to see anything, never once to be in his shortlived presence. Never to see him standing before me as a person, to have him by me as a brother. To go with him through life without seeing him, without (humanly speaking) being able to hold his hand in mine, without once being able to express the tenderness of my feelings, without once being able to look into his eyes... Recently my prayer has become terrifyingly matter-of-fact.' Such letters from people in search of God are legion. It seems to be a basic law of the spiritual life. God never shows himself. Therefore there are people who claim that God does not exist and never has existed. Anyone who does not seek the Giver but only the gift will always be disappointed by God; but anyone who really seeks God will also be able to enjoy God's gifts. If we really seek God, then it will be a matter of asking restlessly 'Warm or cold?', and yet never finding the hidden treasure. The psalmist expresses this poetically: 'My soul thirsts for God, for the living God. When shall I come and behold the face of God? My tears have been my food day and night, while men say to me continually, "Where is your God?" By day I continue to look to the Lord for his grace and by night my song resounds as a prayer to the living God. I say to God my rock, "Why have you forgotten me?"' (Ps.42).

In her love letters the Flemish mystic Hadewijch writes: 'When will you give me the light of day, and a change from my darkness? How glad I'd be to see the sun' (*Poems in Stanzas*, 19,7), and then she goes on: 'Love shows itself as it were in flight; one follows it, but it remains unseen.' And then she concludes: 'That makes the heart stronger and stronger every day' (40th song). In the light of this we also understand the frequent lament in the Old Testament: 'No one can see God without dying' (Exod.33.18-20; Judg.13.22; Isa.6.2).

The one who seeks God seeks the Giver in all gifts. That is the ascesis of the person who is really in search of God; an obstinate refusal to confuse God with any creature whatever: with an experience, with an insight, a feeling, an apostolic work, a book that one writes about God. It is a diffident refusal to confuse God with our prayer, with our ascesis or fasting; full of hesitation, a refusal to confuse God with the gifts of the Holy Spirit. '*Si vere quaeris Deum*', if you are really in search of God, you must reconcile yourself to living in religious darkness. Granted, life is similarly darkness for those who think that they are in search of God but are really in search of themselves, but in that case it is a darkness which sows unrest, arouses discontent and displeasure.

It is striking that when Jesus wrestled on the cross with the silence of God as expressed in the psalm, 'My God, my God, why have you forsaken me?', one may also think of the closing verses of this psalm: 'Those who seek the Lord shall praise him' (Ps.22.27). Does the living God not listen to our life story with the utmost interest and in silence all our life long until we have expressed ourselves wholly and each person has communicated his or her own life to God? Silence is an element of any conversation or any dialogue. Now what is a human life before the eternal God? A second in his divine life. A sigh, a moment in which we can only say a few words to the listening God; therefore God can answer only when our fleeting life on earth is ended. We must let God be God, give God time to listen to our story. We too do not like people constantly interrupting before we have finished! Because God is greater than our human heart, God never comes as a human voice into the depths of our being but as a divine silence, a silence which only becomes a voice and a visible face after our death.

However, all this also has a counterpart in practice. A mediaeval abbot once asked a postulate who had fled to the cloister out of a perverse attitude of renunciation: 'Mon ami, avez vous jamais été amoureux?' Have you never been in love? Whereupon the postulant hastily replied, 'Oh non?! Jamais, mon Père!' No, no, never. And elegantly and laconically the abbot remarked: 'Comment donc voulez-vous aimer le Créateur, si vous n'avez même pas été capable d'aimer une créature?' How will you love the Creator if you have never been capable of loving a creature? Let us reflect on that for a moment here, silently and self-critically.

22

Doubt in God's omnipotence: 'When bad things happen to good people'

Introduction

We have only human words for talking about God and his omnipotence, words which are only suitable for talking about human and worldly things; we do not have a divine language. Therefore if we are to be able to speak about God, we must metaphorically rebaptize and extend all our words. Above all the word 'power' has been seriously infected by human activity. Human power can certainly also be liberating and productive, but it is often destructive and enslaving, imprisoning and manipulative. Precisely because we usually experience relationships of power in this sense, modern men and women are wary about using the term 'omnipotence' of God; it conjures up too much the dictatorial power which enslaves men and women. And the wariness about using the term 'omnipotence' of God applies all the more when it becomes clear that in the course of history Christian churches have flocked to the side of the 'powerful of this world' and in a religious context, too, have treated as nobodies and enslaved those who were already poor and oppressed in society, often with a reference to God's omnipotence. So if we speak of God's omnipotence, it must be of a liberating omnipotence, a good omnipotence. Otherwise it is better not to use such words in connection with God.

The word 'defencelessness' or 'impotence' does not indicate precisely what the 'defenceless superior power'[1] of God really means either. But human experiences of defencelessness and vulnerability allow believers to expect God to be present among vulnerable and defenceless men and women and also to make himself vulnerable along with them. That is certainly one aspect of the problem that we are discussing, even a comforting one. However, we shall soon see that this is not enough to bear the full weight of the problem.

In asking whether God is omnipotent or powerless we shall have to avoid four possible approaches.

1. We cannot talk about God's omnipotence in the abstract, as in speculative mediaeval trains of thought. If we do, we arrive at the craziest questions like: can God make a square circle? Can he make the past never have happened? Can he create a world in which there is no evil and suffering? Moreover, such questions and possible answers have never been much use to anyone. When God is involved, so too are the salvation and happiness of men and women. So anyone who asks about God's omnipotence or helplessness without at the same time asking about human salvation is already on the wrong lines and occupied with pseudo-problems.

Peter de Rosa, a Briton who has produced many scripts for religious programmes on the BBC, wrote a short but sensitive book, a kind of reverse parable of the creation story.[2] God wants to create the best of worlds, in which there is no suffering and no evil, nothing that can cause irritation. You see him drawing up his blueprints: always perfect creaturely beings. According to the plan nothing can go wrong. And indeed in reality everything goes without a snag. But imperceptibly, in the long run there is a stir among these perfect creaturely robots: they rebel against God, they want some adventure, something that cannot be forecast, a risk; they want to venture something with the chance of suffering and things going wrong, with the chance even of eventual success or total fiasco. In any case all creatures ask for an 'adventurous life' in which life and death have a place and not a pre-programmed computer world which does not mean anything. And God finally sees that he was wrong in making a perfect human world.

Selma Lagerlöf, a Scandinavian novelist who was accused of writing only about human evil and suffering and not about the good, replied: 'Don't you know, only evil makes history?' The good is so obvious that you have nothing to say about it. It even *is* gratuitous. But evil has a very turbulent history.

2. Nor can we think along the lines of the popular book by the American rabbi Harold S.Kushner, *When Bad Things Happen to Good People*.[3] This book has rightly comforted many people; for many people it has rightly done away with the idea that God is tormenting and nagging them with suffering for their own good. But one of the basic presuppositions of this book is that God has absolutely nothing to do with human evil and suffering: he stands above and outside them. It is true that God does not want evil or human suffering, and that must be emphasized and repeated, but that does not mean that God has nothing to do with them. Kushner's answer is too easy and too superficial.

3. A while ago, above all in North America, some theologians

wanted to seek the solution in a theology which took the 'death of God' as a starting point: the process of history liberates people from the oppressive figure of the omnipotent God. God has to die so that man may live (T.Altizer). The mistake of this theology lies in the fact that it makes the absence of God in the Western secularized world a normative theological concept without analysing the social and historical reasons for this absence, namely the context of exploitation and annexation of property for the benefit of a few. By means of Western power Christianity has made God play the role of an oppressor: it has transposed its own cultural, economic and political imperialism to God and forgotten the subversive figure of Jesus of Nazareth. However, the God of Jesus is a God who is involved in the history of the struggle against all oppressive power.

4. After people had been talking for centuries about the omnipotence of God, in the last forty years, beginning with Bonhoeffer, stress began to be laid on the defencelessness and the powerlessness of God. Facts like Auschwitz have become a symbol for the defencelessness of God. People began to put the emphasis on a God who shares in suffering, a God who endures suffering along with the poor and oppressed. That may be true, and I too shall put emphasis on it, but it is not enough: in this way it does not become clear *to what extent*, *how* and above all *whether* God is still a redeeming and liberating God. A God who only shares our suffering leaves the last and definitive word to evil and suffering. In that case not God but evil is the definitive omnipotence. And in that case what does God mean for men and women? So we shall have to look in a different direction from these four approaches.

The starting point for our talk about God

To talk meaningfully about God is possible only on the basis of human experience. For Christians, the basis of talk about God – alongside the general basis of their involvement in this, our created world, in experience and interpretation – is above all (and specifically) Israel's experience of God and Jesus of Nazareth, an experience affirmed in faith, which from God's side is called 'revelation'. And this experience was handed down in an interplay of interpretation and new experiences. Not fifty years ago, but now, we in fact raise the question whether God is omnipotent, whereas people formerly took that as a matter of course or proclaimed it in a purely authoritarian way. For our human experience in the second half of the twentieth century this omnipotence is no longer so obvious. Does the whole history of humanity not tell against this omnipotence? Does not Auschwitz – as the symbol of so much satanic evil in our history – tell against this omnipotence? Or all the innocent suffering and injustice in this world, or the distress of the Third World? Or, if we look on a smaller scale: does not the dashing to pieces of just one innocent baby tell against God's omnipotence?

If we should answer such questions and cries only by saying that God's omnipotence will only appear in the end-time, above history – one day all the evil of this world will be overcome in a post-earthly existence – then we must take into account the fact that the more time goes on, above all Western Europeans in a '*fin de siècle*' mentality are getting increasingly weary of the question of the messianic future with its excessive expectations; they seem to be dissociating themselves from the ideas of the 1960s that there must be a positive link between the kingdom of God and the beginning of the overcoming of evil here and now, already in our world (I experience that among fellow theologians). And yet I would have thought that for a Christian it must be clear that there is a positive link between the kingdom of God and the kingdom of human freedom!

If here and now we *nowhere* experience where and how God's power is at work against evil, belief in God's omnipotence is sheer ideology, a loose statement without the possibility of any verification or any meaning. I want to discuss that problem here. But first, in a brief historical survey, I shall outline how this problem arose in the tradition of Christian religious experience.

A brief historical survey

Although the so-called Apostles' Creed begins with the confession of God's omnipotence, 'I believe in God, the Father Almighty, maker of heaven and earth', it would be a great mistake to think that the omnipotence of God is central to the Old and New Testaments. Quite the contrary; the history of God with Israel is to a large degree the history of someone who constantly sees his plans failing and who has constantly to react afresh, tactically and strategically, to the disobedient initiative of his partner, without evidently having the power or the will to compel this partner to do his will. Evil seems so to have the upper hand that in Genesis 6.6 God himself says that he 'regrets' having created this humankind, given the abundance of evil and suffering that it has caused in the good creation. And in the New Testament things are no better. There we are confronted with the worst nadir of all: the Messiah who was to bring salvation to the world hangs defenceless on the cross. There, free but rebellious human beings triumph, while Jesus, the bringer of salvation, cannot or will not free himself, and his God maintains complete silence.

Only in the Greek translation of the Old Testament does the use of the term *pantocrator*, ruler of all, for God come to the fore. From the patristic period onward God's omnipotence becomes something that is taken for granted and is never discussed. This tradition is summed up well in the question *de divina potentia* of the *Summa* of St Thomas. But Thomas already recognizes a certain limitation of God's omnipotence: he draws a distinction between God's absolute omnipotence (*potentia absoluta*) by which he can do anything that is meaningful (anything that comes under the *ratio entis*) and on the other hand his power conditioned by the creation (*potentia ordinata*),[4] in which he takes account of the actual nature of all created things, the distinctive nature of things and persons.

Some centuries later Humanism and the Renaissance laid greater weight on human freedom and autonomy than in the Middle Ages. The consequence of this was that from the end of the sixteenth century to the nineteenth century enormous tensions arose in theology over the relationship between God's omnipotence and human freedom. The central question was whether or not human freedom can limit God's omnipotence. Jesuits and Dominicans got into one another's hair over Molinism, with their views of how these two were to be reconciled, until in 1607 the Pope intervened and for a time banned all polemic on this question.

In the meantime the Reformation encountered the same problem: in particular Remonstrants and counter-Remonstrants fought over the question whether human beings with their free will could or could not withstand God's grace. The Remonstrants seized on Acts 7.51, 'Stubborn and uncircumcised of heart and ear, you always rebel against the Holy Spirit as your fathers did before you', and thus claimed that this was possible. But they were condemned in the Canonical Rules of Dort (III/IV, esp. 10-12). The question was thus whether human beings can develop an initiative of their own to resist God's election to blessedness (the term then used).

With the Enlightenment in the eighteenth century the accent was put even more strongly on humankind come of age, even in respect of God, than at the beginning of modern times. And in that connection people then began to talk about the 'self-limitation' of God; these theologians were called 'kenoticists' on the basis of Philippians 2.7, which mentions a self-emptying or kenosis of God at the incarnation. But among the kenoticists this 'self-emptying' was often understood as a kind of 'self-obliteration' of God, something like an anticipation of the 'death-of-God' theology.

Finally, in a work which has become famous, written in a Nazi prison, Dietrich Bonhoeffer was one of the first to write: 'Only the suffering God can help.'[5] God himself is then seen as a victim of human autonomy and a world come of age. In Christ God dies to human autonomy. Inspired by this, the Dutch *New Catechism* of 1966 associated the confession of God's omnipotence with the confession of God who suffers and fights in a world of becoming and sin.[6] Those are the main lines of a historical survey.

The defencelessness of God

I would prefer to speak, not of the impotence or powerlessness of God but of his defencelessness, because power and powerlessness contradict one another, whereas defencelessness need not *per se* contradict God's power. We know from experience that those who make themselves vulnerable can sometimes disarm evil! I want gradually to give content to this term of God's vulnerability on three different levels: God's defencelessness at creation; God's defencelessness in his Messiah Jesus Christ; and the defencelessness of the Holy Spirit in the church and in the world.

1. The defenceless creator of heaven and earth

We are created in God's image. To be created is, on the one hand, to be taken up as a creature into God's absolute free and saving nearness, but on the other hand, seen from God's side, it is a sort of 'divine yielding', giving room to the other. This non-godly, protected room of one's own is necessary if God is to make this other his covenant partner. True partnership presupposes a contribution, freedom, and initiative from both sides; otherwise there is no partnership! By giving creative space to human beings, God makes himself vulnerable. It is an adventure full of risks. Daring to call human beings to life creatively is from God's perspective a *vote of confidence in humankind* and *in its history*, without any condition being placed on human beings or any guarantee being asked of them. The creation of human beings is a blank check for which God alone is a guarantor. By creating human beings with their own finite and free will, God voluntarily renounces power. That makes him to a high degree dependent on human beings and thus vulnerable.

This does not do away with the saving presence of God, his immanence in creation. But this creative power of God never breaks in from outside. His power is inwardly present; Augustine even says *interior intimo meo*. God is more intimate in me than I am identical with myself. Therefore the divine omnipotence does not know the destructive facets of the human exercising of power, but in this world it becomes defenceless and vulnerable. It shows itself as a power of love which challenges, gives life and frees human beings, at least those who hold themselves open to this offer. But at the same time that means that God does not retaliate against this human refusal.

The sin in the world of creation in fact makes the Creator defenceless in the extreme. Moreover the rule of evil seems universal and ineradicable in our history; the theory of original sin bears witness that Catholicism too, and not just the Reformation, has laid stress on the degree of sinfulness in our world. If human beings prefer to use their freedom to remove themselves from the communion with God intended by him and from mutual human solidarity; in other words, if people use the freedom and room given by God for themselves, they make themselves adversaries of God and put limits on God's power. 'Behold, I stand at the door and knock,' says the book of Revelation (3.20): God stands on the threshhold and knocks at the door, but if we do not freely open it, he does not come in. Out of respect for our freedom he refuses to force the door of our heart and our free will. But he continues to be present in redemption and forgiveness: he does not go away, and continues to knock. In other words, this limit is not God's limit but our limit: the limit of our finitude and above all the limit of our free sinfulness. But God is also present to save beyond this limit, if necessary as the final judge. Meanwhile he is indeed defenceless.

2. *The defenceless God who liberates and redeems*

The nadir of the defencelessness of the redeeming God is manifested in the death of Jesus on the cross. But there we also have the divine mode of 'omnipotence' revealed in the best possible way. In my *Jesus* book I investigated what made possible the origin of the resurrection faith. For Christian faith began with a hopeless defeat. In the meantime it has struck me that at the moment of the deepest disappointment (Jesus' execution – and on the shameful cross) a liberating faith could break through in a cry of victory: 'He lives!', 'He is risen!', and that was not a kind of desperate *Deus ex machina* or some piece of *hocus pocus*.

What did these first disciples, then, really see and experience as the power of God when they saw the powerless defencelessness of their beloved master on the cross, mocked and unrecognized, hissed at and outcast? God was silent when Jesus hung on the cross: he did not come to save his Messiah sensationally. And some days later these disciples came to say cheerfully that Jesus had won through, that 'he lives'. How did they discover that in Jesus' defencelessness the grace of God seemed to have been victorious despite everything? The answer to this question will occupy us shortly.

3. *The defencelessness of the Holy Spirit in the church and in the world*

Even after the 'triumph' of Easter, the history of evil goes on its usual way, as though no redemption had been brought by Christ. On the contrary, the churches, which are the sign of this redemption among us, are themselves often on the side of the powerful of this world and have contributed to the fact that above all in the West, faith in God is associated with systems of political and economic exploitation.

In the light of this, the most urgent question is not that of the presence or absence, the omnipotence or defencelessness, of God, but of the *function* that the symbol God has in a given society. If this function is liberating, then it is responsible and effective along the line of the gospel. If it is oppressive, then it has to be challenged.

God's defenceless superior power

If we stop at God's defencelessness, we have given only half a solution to the problem raised. No answer has been given to the question whether our God is still a saving God. Alongside God's defencelessness we must set his superior power.

To begin with, any meaningful answer that is given to this must be of such a nature that Jesus' death (and certainly his shameful death) is not trivialized in the light of the resurrection. Jesus' death is historically in fact a process of defencelessness. To talk of Jesus' atoning death or of the redemptive value of this death can become sheer ideology. Paul says that the cross is not a sign of honour but a curse (Gal.3.13), a scandal, ignominy: and the resurrection of Jesus does not remove this. In Jesus' death in and of itself there is only negativity. In his case this is not an instance of ordinary death nor of the universal human problem of death, or of the dialectic between death and life, as Bultmann argues, but an ignominious execution which is quite out of proportion to the actual career of Jesus – it is even in flagrant contradiction to it. Thousands are crucified, and nevertheless their crucifixion is not thought to be of universal significance nor called an atoning death. So it cannot lie in Jesus' death, nor even in his crucifixion as such. For this reason the death of Jesus cannot have any redemptive or liberating value: on the contrary, death is the enemy of life. So Jesus' saving worth cannot lie in his death *qua* death.

My position is therefore that if Jesus' career does not show any anticipatory characteristics of the resurrection, his death is sheer failure and belief in the resurrection is indeed (as Jacques Pohier thinks) simply the fruit of human longing. Without effective anticipations of the resurrection in the life of Jesus, Easter is an ideology. The only subject of the statement of faith that 'He is risen' is the historical Jesus of Nazareth who believed in the promise by giving it form in his message and above all in his way of life. Jesus' faith in the promise as the source of an original praxis is a historical anticipation of the meaning of the resurrection and thus God's superior power over evil. In his life Jesus is an 'already', albeit still within the horizon of death, but in that case it is a death which is already overcome in hope. The power of God was already effective in the very life of Jesus and his death shares in that. Only on this presupposition is faith in the resurrection not an ideology! If only Jesus' death (as is the case above all for Bultmann and to some degree already for the apostle Paul) is a historical anticipation of his resurrection, this resurrection is unavoidably the negation of a history in which sin is the sting and death is the consequence.

So we cannot detach the defencelessness of Jesus on the cross from the free power and the positivity that manifested itself in his actual career of solidarity with oppressed people on the basis of an absolute trust in God. God is concerned with a happy existence for people who live under the threat of nature and above all of social oppression. Jesus is so dedicated to this that his concern for his own survival fades into the background here and even plays no role at all. Oppression may not be; the right of the strongest may not apply in the life of human beings one with another. Oppression is injustice and a scandal. So Jesus refuses to regard evil as being on the same footing as good and acts accordingly. Jesus' career itself is therefore praxis of the kingdom of God, a historical anticipation of the resurrection, and his death is part of this career. So we can speak of his death as defenceless superior power, the disarming of evil. It was, moreover, already an insight of the first Christians that the earthly life of Jesus must already show positive anticipations of the resurrection if belief in the resurrection is not to be ideological; and this insight is pointedly expressed in the story in which the Synoptic Gospels speak of a transfiguration of Jesus during his earthly life.

So we can understand why it is precisely at the moment of the deepest disappointment, on the cross, that a liberating belief could break through among the disciples. This is also the heart of the answer to the problem of God's power and defencelessness. Let us analyse the content of this in detail.

The psalm which Jesus prays on the cross and which begins with the words 'My God, my God, why have you forsaken me' ends in a prayer of thanksgiving for God's abiding, albeit silent, saving presence. God was not powerless when Jesus hung on the cross, but defenceless, vulnerable, as Jesus was vulnerable. The basic experience of the first disciples after Good Friday was: no, evil, the cross, cannot have the last word. Jesus' way of life is right and is the last word, that is sealed in his resurrection. Although the cross was on the one hand the sealing of the superior power of humankind over God, God is present in the dying Jesus and is so as pure positivity, as he was in the living Jesus. Suffering and death then remain absurd and may not be mystified, even in Jesus' case; but they do not have the last word, because the liberating God was absolutely near to Jesus on the cross, as he was during the whole of Jesus' career. However, that was a presence without power or compulsion.

Paul says that 'the foolishness of God is wiser than men and the weakness of God is stronger than men' (I Cor.1.25): God was close and present in power, but without misusing power. So God can be present in reconciliation and we may speak of the redemptive and liberating career and death of Jesus. God *conceals* his superior power over evil and *expresses it at the same time* in his defencelessness, in order to give us room to become ourselves in solidarity with oppressed men and women. However, in this defencelessness at the same time he uses his superior power so that his defencelessness is the consequence of his fight against evil in an evil world. The messianic 'must suffer' of Jesus is not a 'divine' must: it is forced on God by human beings through Jesus; nevertheless God and Jesus are not checkmated by it. No, it is not by virtue of the resurrection as such, which would then be regarded as a sort of compensation for the historical failure of the message and praxis of Jesus. It was because his 'going round Palestine doing good' was itself already the beginning of the kingdom of God, of a kingdom in which death and injustice no longer have a place. In Jesus' praxis of the kingdom of God his resurrection is already anticipated. The Easter faith asserts that murder has no future: precisely for that reason death is overcome. The crucified one is also the risen one: that is 'defenceless superior power'.

Experience of God's defenceless superior power in the Christian life

Just as positive anticipations of the resurrection and thus of the victory of grace must be demonstrable in Jesus' life, so one must also argue that for Christians it must be possible to experience the superior power of God within the defencelessness of their own lives; otherwise one would be accepting it on the basis of a purely authoritarian faith.

Anyone who begins to look for this element of present experience must, I think, first be well aware of the difference between our time-conditioned existence and God's eternity. As human beings, we know that silence is an element of any dialogue, of any talking. Now how is that to be understood in a dialogue between human beings and God? What is a human life of at most between seventy and ninety years to the eternal God? A fraction in his divine life; a sigh, a moment in which we can say barely a few words to the listening God. Therefore God is silent in our earthly life. He listens to what we have to say to him. God can only answer when our fleeting life on earth is ended. Should the living God not be extremely interested in us all our lives, listen silently to our life story until we have expressed everything and each person has communicated his or her own life to God? Do not we too dislike being constantly interrupted before we have finished? Nor does God interrupt us, but for him the whole of our life, however important, is just a breath. And God also takes it seriously; that is why he is silent: he is listening to our life story. Precisely because he is greater than our human heart, he never speaks as a tangible human voice in our innermost being but only as a 'divine silence', a silence that only after our death takes on a distinctive voice and face that we can recognize. As long as the Eternal One is still listening to our life story of fifty or even a hundred years, the eternal God indeed seems to us to be powerless and defenceless.

We human beings live, speak and act for perhaps a hundred years – God for his part, however, keeps silent (by comparison, calculating in human terms) for just a second, in order to let us speak.

In this there is both a desperate trial for our historical existence and at the same time an experience full of hope and expectation.

Looking in this light for experience of God's defenceless victory, one can argue that however great and stubborn the kingdom of evil is, good is *more original* than evil. We Christians can make this an explicit theme on the basis of our belief in creation, but one can also demonstrate it by experiences which are common to all human beings. I would like to illustrate by a rather extreme example that the resurrection faith not only stresses our responsibility for the world but even becomes an ideology if that faith has no historical anticipations in a praxis of actual opposition to evil and injustice.

Imagine that in a dictatorship a soldier in a firing squad is ordered to shoot dead an innocent hostage, purely and simply because, for example, he is a Jew, a Communist or a Christian. He refuses to carry out the order for reasons of conscience. He is certain that he himself will then be shot along with this hostage (who will be shot by someone else). But in his refusal the soldier recognizes that the humiliated bewilderment of the hostage is an unspoken and perhaps inexpressible moral summons which he experiences as a demand. The other lays claim on his freedom: he experiences the ethical impossibility of his killing this man and therefore refuses to carry out the order.

In this act of conscience which on the one hand (as Levinas puts it)[7] demonstrates 'the end of the powers' by the disarming death of the soldier, there is on the other hand something paradoxical, something which even lies on the border of the absurd. For the moral gesture of the soldier is not only to be regarded as ineffective as far as the life of the hostage is concerned (someone else shoots him) but also means the immediate end of his own life with all its unrealized possibilities (he too is shot). So the soldier seems to be under an ethical demand which is at the same time beyond question absurd. That is defencelessness to the nth degree and yet in it lies 'the end of the powers'!

That the other person is an ethical demand on me thus leads to an aporia: on the one hand there is no guarantee that evil – violence and injustice, torture and death – will not have the last word over our finite experiences of the world, and on the other there is a certain absurdity: an evidently useless gesture which seems to help no one. Two ethically honest 'solutions' to this aporia are possible. On the one hand one can talk of a 'heroic act', as Sartre or Camus would do in this case: a gratuitous heroic action for the sake of the *humanum*. On the other hand the reply could go in a religious direction, albeit equally on the basis of human values. Both solutions conjure up a vision of reality by holding fast to the *humanum* – the specific person in his or her invulnerability – human beings becoming victims of empirical factuality, but at the same time putting it to shame. On the basis of someone's positive answer to another's ethical appeal, against all the appearances, the gratuitous action gains the victory over the empirical triumph of the facts. In both cases we have to do with hope for the ultimate victory of the good: faith in human beings despite everything. But in that case the question has to be asked: what is this hope founded on? What are the theoretical truth-conditions of this hope?

In the religious answer God himself is the ground of hope and there is well-founded hope. But what are the grounds for the non-religious, humanistic hope in the final victory of good over the apparent empirical triumph of actual evil? Just a 'postulatory' hope, a hope that is positivistically postulated against all hope by our own free will? That can be courageous and brave, but is it wishful thinking? Belief in humanity despite everything cannot be a mere positivistic act of will, for in that case people would be trying to drag themselves out of the mire by their own hair. The possibility of a total, emancipatory self-liberation is contradicted by the fact that men and women are not only grace to their fellow human beings but also threat, violence and annihilation, time and again, sometimes with refined technical means. To say that martyrdom is not in vain and that coming generations will reap the fruits of this earlier suffering may be true for some, or even many, people. But the case of the soldier can repeat itself time and again in the future. So while one can indeed interpret the soldier's refusal in a secular sense, as a prophetic action in hope of the eventual triumph of humanity, in that case one must be aware that there are no grounds for this hope in history or anthropology. Is it a postulatory hope? Of course such hope can have beneficial historical effects. The brave action of the soldier is capable of articulating and mobilizing the aspirations of an important group of people in society.

But one may not make too absolute a contrast between the humanistic-agnostic and the religious interpretation of such a martyrdom. The humanistic hope is not just a postulate; it has a foundation in an autonomous ethical conviction. At any rate one can argue that there is hope for the triumph of the human, because the sacrifice of the soldier knows that it has justice on its side, and that it is not on the side of those in power. The human conviction that justice is superior to injustice in fact gives grounds for such a hope. However, this human conviction is just as true for believers and forms the mediation of their faith in God. Religions and agnostic humanism continue to trust that justice is greater than injustice and evil. According to the testimony of Simone de Beauvoir, the agnostic Jean-Paul Sartre, at one time even a militant atheist, said on his deathbed: 'And yet I continue to trust in the humanity of humankind.' The humanistic hope is thus not purely postulatory; the conviction that one is on the side of justice provides grounds for this expectation; the hope is founded on the rightness of justice, despite the fact that the experienceable world is constantly an empirical contradiction of this. However, the humanist does not know in the end whether reality itself will prove our ethical conviction of standing on the side of justice to be right.

The great difference from the religious view is thus that hope with a purely ethical foundation offers a perspective on perhaps a higher degree of humanity for some or even many people in the future, but forgets the many sacrifices which have been made and the countless victims who will still fall. The fallen themselves then experience no liberation or redemption; they have lived so that in the future other people may perhaps not have to undergo the same fate.

In the experience in faith of this extreme ethical situation the person who believes in God sees and experiences reality with its absolute limitation in the last resort not as a blind faith or as a wild chance, but as being in fact personal, namely supported by God's absolute saving presence.

In situations which are not willed by God nor even tolerated by him but which are in fact absurd, God is nevertheless near to bring salvation. The absurd is not argued away, far less understood rationally or approved of in religious terms, but for the believer it does not have the last word: believers entrust the absurdity to God, the source of pure positivity and the transcendent foundation of all ethics; the mystical source of any ethical dedication, which still gives hope to the actual victim, who outside the religious perspective is written off for good. It is not that the martyr offers his brave death in order to get 'an eternal reward'. Certainly his or her historical action is itself stronger than death; this act itself is praxis of the kingdom of God and bears within itself the germ of resurrection. The one who believes in God sees faith in the superiority of justice and goodness to all injustice as an experience of the meta-human (for people clearly cannot produce it in their history), an experience of the absolute presence of God's pure positivity in the historical mixture of meaning and meaninglessness which is called the 'human' phenomenon and its history. This is no belittling of the human by making an appeal to a completely alien factor, God. For this appeal to God on the one hand takes the form of the human conviction that justice is superior to all injustice and on the other hand is an appeal precisely not to what is completely alien, but to the ultimate, innermost source of all justice: the intimate presence of the exclusively positive reality, 'God': a God who does not want death but life for his own.

Here we also have a pregnant expression of the fact that for the one who believes in God, above all the Christian, faith in God in one and the same movement frees men and women for love of God and love of their fellow human beings, and above all for love of the maltreated and the outcast (Matt.25.40). This devotion to one's fellow human beings, even to the point of ethical martyrdom, is to be regarded as a context with which human beings can empathize, within which (in a massively secular world) a humanly relevant, philosophically meaningful notion of God's defenceless victory can find a place, and which has its own possibility of being understood that can be recognized by others.

The answer to the ethical appeal sketched out here which is given by both the secular humanist and the person who believes in God thus lies in a gratuitous or 'vain sacrifice', whether in a heroic sense or as a 'vain offering of love' in a deeply human sense of trusting in God in a holy, non-heroic way despite everything. These are two possibilities for human life, both of which have their own honesty and capacity to be understood. For the believer the religious interpretation is the more understandable and the more honest. The non-believer sees more honesty in the agnostic interpretation. But within this context what believers mean by God is understandable even to non-believers. The believer finds sufficient signs of this faith in his or her human experience, and does so without these experiences losing human reality.

The most obvious way to understand something of the defenceless superior power of God in our day is to give a warm welcome to our fellow human beings in this our wicked world, both on an interpersonal level and by changing the structures which enslave human beings, men and women. Theology is then reflection in faith on the praxis of justice and love. What is at stake here is not simply the *ethical consequence* of the religious or theologal life; rather, ethical praxis becomes an essential component of a life directed to God, of 'the true knowledge of God': 'He judged the cause of the poor and needy; then it was well. Is not this to know me? says the Lord' (Jer.22.16). God is accessible above all in the praxis of justice and love. 'No one has ever seen God; if we love one another, God abides in us and his love is perfected in us' (I John 4.12).

If liberation is the real hallmark of the power of good, then for anyone who consistently continues to regard the world from the standpoint of the victims and thus from solidarity with these victims, this solidarity, if it inspires all action, is a power which is literally stronger than death, a power which disarms evil and makes it yield. Among human beings who – in more and more countries – are tortured and executed and then bear witness to their solidarity with the poor and oppressed, this seems as large as life in our days. Defencelesness can indeed dethrone powers and show the superiority of humanity over all that is inhuman and in so doing, for believers, show the superior power of God.

That this position is right can never be proved, but many people will want to *bear witness* to it. Non-Christians can also bear witness to the same experience. However, in it Christians find the definitive truth of God's power. 'God is as strong and as weak as love'![8]

Notes

1. For H.Berkhof, 'defenceless superior power' is one of God's properties, see *Christian Faith*, Eerdmans 1986, section 22, p.140.
2. Peter de Rosa, *The Best of All Possible Worlds*, Argus Communications 1976.
3. H.S.Kushner, *When Bad Things Happen to Good People*, Pan Books and Schocken Books 1981.
4. Thomas Aquinas, *Summa Theologiae* I, q.25 ad 1.
5. D.Bonhoeffer, *Letters and Papers from Prison*, ed. E.Bethge, SCM Press and Macmillan, New York 1971, 361.
6. *A New Catechism. Catholic Faith for Adults*, Burns and Oates/Herder and Herder 1967, 495-502.
7. See E.Levinas, *Totalité et Infini*, The Hague 1961, 51-9, 291.
8. H.Häring, 'Het kwaad als vraag naar Gods macht en machteloosheid', *Tijdschrift voor Theologie* 26, 1986, (356-72) 371.

23

God as a bogeyman for some Christians

I. The problem

Believers rightly feel that if one says that 'God is love' one cannot regard this love as the kindliness of a grandparent who turns a blind eye to and excuses the naughtiness of little children, even if this naughtiness has long ceased to be mere mischief. That is perhaps the danger of too-nonchalant Catholic talk of 'Our dear Lord' in contrast to the 'Godfearing' Protestant talk of 'the Lord'. On the other hand the imputation of blame or attribution of guilt to people, as when some Protestant Christians often talk about the righteous judge and the punitive justice of God, does not seem to me to be very pleasant. I think that the way in which at present, above all in North America, Evangelicals moralize about 'the wrath of the Lord' and in so doing scare the living daylights out of people, so that as well as producing a flood of tears of repentance they pour an even greater flood of gold, silver and jewels into the hands of the neo-evangelists, is a danger to people's spiritual health. I think that this is above all fatal to a truly religious attitude; at the same time it is a misuse of human weakness and frailty to use a process of imputing guilt to people to make them ripe for what must then be termed the *so-called* grace of God.

But apart from these modern excesses, the talk of great theologians like Karl Barth about Jesus as being at the same time the predestined one and the one rejected by God also seems to me to go beyond all the bounds of the New Testament. The divine violence against humankind would be being undone by directing violence at the innocent one *par excellence*. The violent, retributive justice is then more radical than the kindly gratuitousness of Jesus and in that case Jesus is indeed merely a transitional figure. Here a distortion of Christianity is at work against which we must be on our guard as modern but authentic Christians.

Certainly, although both the first and the second Testaments are full of threatening prophecies about the faithlessness of the people, in these somewhat sombre biblical texts it is not the punitive justice of God which is central but the holiness of God's love. From our side the 'fear of God' and from God's side 'the wrath of God' are such fundamental biblical terms that we cannot argue them away. The song of the thrice-holy God also resounds in our Christian eucharistic celebrations. And although we may omit the Gloria and the Creed from these celebrations, we never leave out the 'Holy, holy, holy', the so-called *trisagion*. Therefore the Bible often speaks of the 'holy' love of God. We rightly do not want to forget the unassailable holiness of the one who is nevertheless the God who loves humankind when we celebrate this love of God for humankind. The problem posed in this way immediately raises a couple of questions.

A first difficulty relates to the language we use to speak of God. Like all the attributes that we assign to God, this too is not a directly accurate way of talking about God but a good analogy. God is love, yes, but his love is not like pure human love. God is just, yes, but his justice is not like purely human justice. Yet the human love and human justice which we experience do indicate the direction in which we can say something meaningful about the love and goodness of God. However, we cannot understand the divine mode of goodness. And here there is a second difficulty. All the divine attributes coincide with the nature of God, and this nature of God is absolute freedom, i.e. pure free self-determination without any conditioning from within or without. We cannot infer from the so-called 'nature of God' whether God will finally pronounce a *verbum irae*, a word of wrath, or a *verbum misericordiae*, a definitive word of mercy, on our evil history; it is an absolutely free act of will on the part of God himself, an act which from eternity coincides with the very being of God.

The fact that all divine properties coincide with God's being does not mean that all these properties are synonymous and that the terms which we use, for example justice and love, can be used interchangeably with reference to God. In that case all talk of God would become an abracadabra, talk in incomprehensible tongues. If God's being is pure freedom, it could be that the problem how mercy and punitive justice can be reconciled in God does not exist, because God opts in sovereign freedom for mercy and does so in a way which leaves intact the inviolable holiness of his love.

From these two possibilities it already seems that the dilemma of how we can reconcile God's punitive justice with his mercy betrays an unhistorical, abstract and purely speculative way of posing the problem: in this form it is a pseudo-problem. Something much deeper is at stake.

We can never arrive through speculation at what divine love, what divine justice really is; we discover that only from the history which

God has with human beings, above all from his dealings with the people of Israel and in a decisive way with Jesus of Nazareth. Above all we should look at the significance of God's good creation and ultimately at the life-style of Jesus, since he above all makes transparent to us how things are with God. This is no digression, but the most direct way of making a meaningful statement about God's love and his punitive justice. Otherwise we are confronted with an insoluble dilemma: the two are not to be reconciled; that is often the tragedy in a constitutional state.

Therefore we must already reckon with the possibility that there can be a divine choice between love and justice. Now from the message and career of Jesus we know that as a human being Jesus opted in complete freedom for mercy and against the social rules of strict justice, which can turn into inhumanity. Therefore Jesus freely opts for ultimate mercy and not for 'the vengeance and wrath of God'. If for Christians Jesus is the definitive revelation of God, we must turn to the story of the New Testament to shed light on the nature of God as mercy.

II. Jesus relativizes the rules of social justice

The difference between the message of John the Baptist and that of Jesus, who was initially his disciple, is immediately striking. In the case of John the Baptist, too, message and lifestyle are closely connected. John knows himself to be a prophet, but a prophet of God's approaching judgment: the axe is already laid to the root of the trees. 'You brood of vipers! Who warned you to flee from the wrath to come? Every tree that does not bear good fruit is cut down and thrown into the fire' (Luke 3.7-9; Matt.3.7-10). The future with which the preaching of John the Baptist is concerned is the threatening judgment of the divine judge, God's anger, his inexorable judgment. This is an extremely sharp proclamation.

When Jesus had himself baptized by John, initially he seems to have followed the Baptist's preaching. But according to the synoptic account, after this he spent forty days in retreat in the wilderness. We understand from the story of the three temptations that Jesus had come to a deliberate choice: for mercy and against all apocalyptic, messianic, violent appearances of a Messiah who would reverse conditions and destroy all former oppressors. So Jesus' own mission does not match what his forerunner says of him. Jesus does not want to appear as a judge with an axe already in his hand. Jesus indeed accepts the title of prophet, but does not set himself up as a prophet of doom. On the contrary. The message of Jesus clearly has quite a different accent. 'Kingdom of God' and 'renewal of life' are the two key words of Jesus' message and praxis, summarized in the Gospel of Mark: 'Jesus said: "The time is fulfilled and the kingdom of God is at hand: repent and believe in the Good News"' (Mark 1.15) of the approaching kingdom. *Kingdom of God* is a biblical expression for the nature of God – unconditional and liberating sovereign love – in so far as this is implemented and revealed in the life of men and women who do God's will. The approach of that kingdom is closely connected with *metanoia* or the renewal of human life. Jesus' disciples experienced that with Jesus the kingdom of God had come near to them in and through their own renewal of life; through their faith in Jesus the whole of their life was changed: they had left behind their boats and nets, the source of their livelihood, and followed Jesus on his preaching journeys.

Kingdom of God is a term which does not come naturally to us modern Westerners. Most Western countries are no longer kingdoms. Moreover Christians do not feel bound to the term, although they continue to use it for its evocative power. For Jesus, 'God's kingdom' or 'God's rule' in any case means the saving presence of God among men and women, affirmed or welcomed, active and encouraging, a presence which becomes tangible to all in justice and peaceful relations among individuals and peoples, in the disappearance of sickness, injustice and oppression; in the forgiveness of sins. The kingdom of God is a new world from which suffering has been removed, a world of those who are healed or completely whole in a society in which master-servant relationships no longer prevail, in complete contrast to conditions under Roman occupation; what goes on there 'shall not be so among you' (Mark 10.42-43; Matt.20.25-26; Luke 22.24-27). The rule *of God* over a people is 'liberating' for that people and ultimately even liberating and redeeming on all sides. According to this religious vision people experience the kingdom of God in the experience of their own redemption, salvation and liberation; in the experience of salvation.

The kingdom of God is a converted (*metanoia*), new relationship of men and women to God, and its tangible and visible sign is a new type of liberating relationship among men and women, within a reconciled society in a peaceful ecological setting. However, this kingdom is 'eschatological', i.e. it is there in a fragmentary way in history, but not capable of complete realization. The approach of that kingdom, its anticipatory realization, must take place now, already, within our history. It is precisely here that Jesus preceded his disciples: the inauguration of the kingdom of God already took place in his earthly career (and not just at the resurrection).

It is striking above all in Jesus' parables how he relativizes the absolute of the principle of justice. There are parables which have the aim (then as now) of shocking our sense of justice. The one who works from the eleventh hour gets just as much as the one who works from the first hour (Matt.20.1-17), and from someone who has nothing, even what he has shall be taken away (Matt.25.29). Jesus wants us to learn from this that the rules for the praxis of the kingdom of God have nothing to do with the social rules in our societies. *It is an alternative mode of action.* Jesus does not defend immoral or anarchic people, he goes and stands next to them. He unmasks the intentions of those who are zealous for God and justice; he takes from the zealots even what they have, a zeal for God and the law which excludes human beings; he points to the perverse effects of virtue, like that of the oldest brother of the prodigal son (Luke 15.11-32), who makes arrogant comments about the prodigality of his youngest brother. Jesus reacts sharply against those who uphold the social rules. Strict justice can even include the excommunication of those who have already been cast out. The coming of the kingdom of God does not know the human logic of precise justice. Jesus wants to give hope to those who from a social and human point of view, according to our human rules, have no more hope.

A certain kind of virtuousness and perfection has a subtle character which murders people: particular monastic reactions in 'old-style' monastic life were sometimes full of the subtle vice of the moralizing 'perfection' of particular religious which accused others. In some quarters the subtle vice of this 'perfection' has still not disappeared from church life. People defend so-called unassailable laws and in so doing hurt their already wounded fellow men and women. That puts Jesus to shame. The effects of this zeal are often that people get no room to breathe. Jesus opposes worldly practice when the law has the effect of excluding the other. If the law reduces people to despair, it is deprived of all authority. For Jesus, the poor and outcast are the criterion whether the law, as the will of God for the benefit of men and women, is functioning creatively or destructively.

For Jesus, even the tradition of his Jewish people, of Israel, is not the last authority. This tradition has a human legitimacy for him, but he does not subject himself to it unconditionally.

The novelty of Jesus' relationship to law, to tradition, to the current images of God, does not derive directly from a transcendent authority which takes the place of Moses; in that view whatever new feature emerges in Jesus is derived, without any mediation, directly from his divinity, and the critical force of his human choice, the reason why he was crucified, is completely trivialized. For Jesus God is not the guarantor of society, of prosperity and the family. Jesus' image of God was shaped by the thirsty, the stranger, the prisoner, the sick, the outcast: he sees God in them (Matt.25). In all his behaviour Jesus rejects justice as an 'absolute imperative' (Matt.20.15-16). According to Jesus justice is not the last word. Jesus takes the side of those without an advocate, but with many accusers, who with their appeal to the law, pointing with their fingers, cast out men and women and thus put one more obstacle in their way.

To a great degree the action of Jesus consisted in establishing social communication, opening up communication above all where excommunication, discrimination and expulsion were officially in force: with regard to public sinners, tax collectors making themselves rich from the poor, the possessed, lepers and so on; all those who were thought to be unclean. These are the ones whom Jesus seeks out, and he eats with them, which was officially forbidden. In all this Jesus is aware that he is acting as God would do. In and through his way of life he relates God's action to men and women. His parables talk of a lost sheep, a lost coin, a lost son. He attracts these problem cases. To fellow-Jews who are irritated at his dealings with unclean people Jesus wants to make clear through his action that God turns to lost and wounded people; Jesus acts as God acts. So in him there is a claim that God himself is present in his action and words. To act as Jesus does is praxis of the kingdom of God and moreover shows what the kingdom of God is: salvation for men and women.

In Jesus' company men and women experienced fullness of life in a way which immeasurably transcended their daily experiences (the so-called miracle stories seek to make that clear). In this context the miracles are the sign of the whole, healed and perfect world of the kingdom of God which becomes present and approaches us in them. To believe in Jesus as the Christ means at root to recognize in confession and in fact that Jesus has an abiding and constitutive significance with relation to the whole approach of the kingdom of God and thus in the all-embracing healing of human beings and making them whole. In essence this is the distinctive, unique relationship of Jesus to the coming kingdom *of God* as salvation of and for human beings, which is what all religions confess him to be.

III. Jesus' sovereign human freedom of decision

According to the Christian perspective, God has revealed himself in Jesus through the non-divine aspect of Jesus' humanity. However, this has been interpreted in very different ways within Christianity. Above all within the 'two-natures' scheme of Pope Leo the Great, people often arrived at a kind of christology of paradox, between the extreme of the human and the extreme of the divine, passing over the actual account in the Gospels. In these theologies of redemption there was often an abstract dialectic between 'weak humanity' (*forma servi*: the form of a slave) and the superior power of God (*forma dei*), in an unhistorical view. This view forgot the sovereign-free decision and choice of Jesus which rejects all ideologies of power and therefore resolutely repudiates any attribution of a Jewish 'messiah' title to himself.

Jesus is not condemned because as a man he had divine pretensions, far less for his weak humanity. It emerges from the whole of the Gospel narrative that he was condemned for his sovereign-free choice of a human lifestyle, which is subversive to anyone who gambles and wagers on power. The authority of his appearance was a challenge and led him to a trial and condemnation: his lifestyle forced the powerful to unmask themselves. He made mock of the perverse effects of a particular zeal for 'God's cause', to the detriment of 'the cause of men and women'. In short, Jesus' clear choice was his refusal of any messianic ideology which on the one hand frees the oppressed but on the other hand mercilessly destroys all oppressors, for at the time this was the generally accepted 'apocalyptic model'!

It emerges from the whole of the New Testament (despite some 'interpretations' in another direction) that Jesus put the stress on the 'gratuitousness' of our redemption and liberation. Many existing theories about our redemption by Jesus Christ rob Jesus, his message and his way of life of their subversive power; even worse, they sacralize violence so that it becomes a reality within God. God is said to ask for a bloody sacrifice which will assuage or calm his sense of justice. First vengeance must be taken on sin, and only then is reconciliation possible. The rejection of Jesus by God is then said to reconcile us with God. That goes against the whole proclamation and career of Jesus. Jesus refused to heal the human violence in our history by 'divine violence'.

It is clear from Jesus' three temptations in the wilderness that he resolutely rejected the Jewish expectation in all his doings. To attempt to reconcile mercy and justice is to attempt to harmonize the irreconcilable. As a human being Jesus opts for mercy and gratuitousness, ignoring the penal sanctions of the oppressors and wicked. People do not seem able to imagine that there can be generosity without any strings attached; people seem to be incapable of imagining that injustice should not be subjected to sanctions. Or is another form of penal immanent justice possible, which leaves God out of account? We must go on to investigate that.

Jesus did not want to be a messianic political leader, but this does not mean that his message and life-style did not have a political significance. I would term actions and words 'subversive' which in fact undermine the authority of social and political institutions. Jesus' basic choice was to refuse power, and so his words and actions take on an unparalleled authority. Though himself accepting exclusion and rejection, Jesus does not seek to be the leader of the outcast. In so doing he wants to stress that being outcast is not a privilege but a perverse effect of an oppressive society. The silence of God when Jesus hung on the cross is on the wavelength of the logic of Jesus' lifetime choice, against messianic power.

Really the Christian view of the eschatological last judgment should have the last word on this question.

IV. *The final eschatological judgment: heaven or hell?*

In the Gospel of Matthew the story of the last judgment mentions not only the ultimate liberation of human beings but also a condemnation: 'Depart from me you cursed, into the eternal fire prepared for the devil and his angels' (Matt.25.41). This in fact derives from the literary genre of apocalyptic, in which whereas the oppressed are raised up, all the oppressors are dragged from their thrones and destroyed.

However, Christianity did not take over all aspects of this apocalyptic model. In fact the resurrection of Jesus did not have any of the effects that were expected by the apocalyptic Jewish visionaries. In order to gloss over the absence of these effects, some Christians began to talk about a 'divine postponement of the parousia' and the eschatological last judgment. Within an apocalyptic horizon one has to talk in this way: in that case the postponement of the annihilation of all oppressors belongs with the ultimate victory of the oppressed, but after Easter (as to the present day) the history of oppression and violence continued as usual. The apocalyptic expectation of retribution on and punishment of the evil and the oppressors was disappointed.

However, Christians see the effect of the Easter event in the light of the gift of the Holy Spirit which brings forgiveness, bestowed by the risen Jesus.

The sending of the Holy Spirit and the forgiveness which is given to us by the crucified and risen Jesus of Nazareth presents us with the problem of what happens to the oppressors in our history. Jesus himself does not talk about sanctions on the oppressors, as apocalyptic did. He breaks this apocalyptic mould; the tradition of Christian experience speaks only of an eschatological judgment. But according to the liberation theologians a liberation which does not already take historical and provisional form is in fact complicity or shared guilt in the violence which continues to permeate our human world after Easter. As Karl Marx already said, the purely eschatological solution can in fact work in an alienating way in our history. It is well known that between the fourteenth and the eighteenth century there was anxiety throughout Europe over the vision of the last judgment: architecture and literature are full of it.

We also have visions of 'permanent suffering', eternal damnation, in the New Testament (e.g. Rev.20.10). Whereas in the same Bible we hear that God comes near to the outcast in Jesus, beside the kingdom of God there will for eternity be a kingdom of the 'condemned and suffering', a kingdom of those definitively outcast from the kingdom of God, a kingdom of people who suffer permanently. And this hellish suffering will continue for ever without any meaningful perspective, because by definition in hell no therapeutic significance can be attributed to it. In that case it is solely the perpetuation of revenge: vengeance and retribution. In this view there will be eternal suffering, albeit that of the oppressor. Some Christians (like Peter Berger) have indeed said: 'There is so much evil crying to heaven that there must be something like a hell.' One could think in that way, perhaps too humanly; can the victims of Hitler and Eichmann happily spend eternity in their company? I understand this reaction. But I myself see it like this. Heaven and hell are in the first place anthropological possibilities. In their situated freedom human beings are in fact in a position to do both good and evil. Both good and evil also have a social dimension which transcends personal choice. But in the end human beings, anthropologically, are capable of a definite choice of either good or evil. In this sense heaven and hell are human possibilities. (Whether there are in fact people who definitively choose evil I do not know: no one can discover that. That verdict belongs only to God.) But on the basis of this human possibility the biblical threats and perspectives on 'heaven and hell' are a meaningful anthropological perspective both therapeutically and pedagogically. Whether this anthropological, internal possibility is also a possibility for God is another matter.

The saying of Thérèse of Lisieux, 'Je crois dans l'enfer, mais je crois qu'il est vide,' I believe in hell but I think that it is empty, is anything but unbiblical! There is also the same problem in various traditions of religious experience: some church fathers talk about a general *apokatastasis* or recapitulation, which means that eventually everyone will be saved and get to heaven. There is also the expression of a similar vision in the doctrine of reincarnation in other religions, that ultimately everyone will be saved. Only the way in which this is imagined is different, as there are differences in the possibilities of understanding it rationally.

But I have my reservations about these somewhat too superficial solutions. To my mind they suggest too cheap a view of mercy and forgiveness; moreover they trivialize the drama of the real course of events in the conflict between oppressed and oppressors, between the good and the evil in our human history. Present-day preaching is silent about hell, eternal threat and judgment; they can no longer be heard in the pulpit, only in modern films. After centuries of an enormous inflation of a threatening proclamation of coming doom we now maintain an uncomfortable silence: there is a universal allergy to ultimate sanctions, indeed already to the death penalty on earth.

I myself see it as follows (though I present this as a plausible hypothesis and thus with some hesitation):

Heaven and hell are asymmetrical affirmations of faith: you cannot regard them on the same level. Christian faith in eternal life in the form of 'heaven' has its foundation not in the Greek affirmation of the immortality of the human soul but in living communion with God in grace (expressed in human solidarity) during earthly life. The bond of life with the living eternal God cannot be destroyed by death. In Jesus God overcomes death for those who anticipate the kingdom of love and freedom in history. So there is a heaven.

But in my view there is no hell, at least not equal and symmetrical to it, like positive and negative on the same level; for the evil and the oppressors certainly punish themselves thoroughly for ever. If living communion with God is the foundation of eternal life, then the absence of living communion with God (not so much through theoretical denial of God as through a lifestyle which radically contradicts solidarity with fellow human beings and precisely in that way rejects God and living communion with God) is at the same time the foundation of non-eternal life for these people. That seems to me to be the second death of the fundamental, definitive sinner (if any such person exists): for him or her, physical death is the end of all existence: that is 'hell'; not sharing in eternal life nor being someone who is tortured eternally either, but no longer existing. That is the biblical 'second death' (Rev.20.6). This sanction is the fruit of one's own behaviour and not a positive act of the punitive justice of God who sends sinners to an eternal hellish fire: there is just no ground for eternal life. These people have resisted God's holiness and are incapable of loving. No one in heaven will ever remember them. While there is said to be joy among the heavenly ones, right next to heaven people are supposed to lie for ever gasping for breath and suffering the pains of hell for ever (however you imagine this – spiritually or physically). That is an unimaginable situation for the God of Jesus as I have learned to know him from the New Testament. On the other hand the idea of the second or definitive death respects God's holiness and his wrath at the evil that is done to the detriment of the poor and the oppressed.

So ultimately no one is excluded from the kingdom of God: in that case there is only the 'kingdom of God', a kingdom of liberated and free people, who do not have next door to them a kingdom of those who have been definitively cast out. There is no shadow kingdom of hell next to the eternally happy kingdom of God. The blessed will be spared the fact that a stone's throw away from their eternal happiness fellow human beings should be tortured for ever through whatever physical or spiritual pains. Dante's 'sorrowful city' alongside the joyful palaces of the heavenly blessed ones is a pedagogical picture: especially destructive oppression and utter evil have no future; they are without hope, on the basis of their own logic. There is nothing present in evil and wickedness which is to be marked out for eternal life. There is nothing here that can be integrated into a kingdom of freedom and love. Through its own emptiness and weightlessness the wicked world which was formerly so powerful and evil disappears by its own logic into absolutely nothing, without the blessed having to feel offended by some barracks next to heaven where their former oppressors are tortured for ever. They already had precisely this experience in their earthly life; to have it a second time, for ever, is sheer blasphemy for them. This seems to me to be the most plausible Christian solution, in contrast to the model by which the Christian tradition has usually proclaimed this insight in the past. But in the past no distinction was made between the rights of God's holiness which were justly defended and the exercising of them in the concrete and definitive fate of stubborn sinners; in other words, people put good and evil on the same level: they forgot the asymmetry of good and evil.

Of course the good also has its own intrinsic logic. But it does not follow from this that we should demythologize heaven in the same way as 'hell' and moreover look for heaven in the joy of virtue on earth without any perspective on an eternal life. Here too there is asymmetry in the relationship of God to evil and to good. As far as evil is concerned there is no need for a transcendent factor; Thomas Aquinas himself dared to apply the term *causa prima* (first cause) to creatures where it was a question of total negativity (*'defectus gratiae prima causa est ex nobis'*, *Summa Theologiae* I-II, q.112, a.3 ad 2). By contrast the good finds its ultimate source (or *causa prima*) in God. The internal logic of evil therefore *terminates* in the finite mortality of human beings, while the internal logic of the good *culminates* in the eternal love of God who sustains the good man and woman (despite their many failings) in death and draws them to him over the boundary which is inherent in humanity.

So there is no future for evil and oppression, while goodness still knows a future beyond the boundary of death. God does not take vengeance: he leaves evil to its own (limited) logic! So there is in fact an eternal difference between good and evil, between the pious and the wicked (the deepest intent of the distinction between heaven and hell), but the pious continue to be spared having to rejoice over the torture of eternal doom inflicted on their fellow human beings. God's unassailable holiness consists rather in the fact that he will not compel anyone to enter the kingdom of heaven as the unique kingdom of liberated and free people. The 'eschaton' or the ultimate is exclusively positive. There is no negative eschaton. Goodness, not evil, has the last word. That is the message and the distinctive praxis of Jesus of Nazareth, whom Christians therefore confess as the Christ.

24

'You are a God of peace' and nevertheless bring the sword

I. He is a God of peace

Our God is a God of peace (Isa.9.6; 45.7; I Thess.5.23; II Thess.3.16; I Cor.14.33; II Cor.13.11; Phil.4.7; Heb.13.20): this is not a chance expression in the Bible nor one that stands alone. It is impossible for us to marginalize these expressions: they belong to the heart of the Jewish and Christian confession.

But there are clearly telling historical facts which raise some serious questions about this Christian gospel.

Let us limit ourselves to some basic facts. A third of the population of the world lives on four-fifths of all the foodstuffs available in our world. Two-thirds of all humankind, however, has to make do with the remaining one-fifth, and that is quite inadequate. Millions of people die of hunger in these circumstances. Given this despair, how can there be peace on earth? Moreover there is no peace. The threat of war and disorder lies not so much in the ideological conflict on the East-West axis as in the tension between poor and rich countries, and in that case, if we are concerned for the future of our human world, we must look more in the direction of the North-South axis.

That is the concrete reality. Let us now also look at 'religious utopias'. Despite everything, these too have their own real worth.

Salvation from God and kingdom of God, grace, redemption and liberation, all these great religious concepts from the Christian tradition are always associated with 'peace'. This peace of God bears a name. Not ours, not that of one peace movement or another, but the name of Jesus, the Christ: 'Jesus Christ is our peace' (Eph.2.14-18; Col.3.15). Moreover Christians must also be 'ready to serve the gospel of peace' (Eph.6.15). They must 'strive for peace with all men and women and for a holy life, for without that no one will see the Lord' (Heb.12.14). Peace has something to do with 'seeing God'! So Christians are admonished: 'Have salt in yourselves and be at peace with one another' (Mark 9.49-50), or even: 'Strive for justice, faith, love and peace' (II Tim.2.22).

In short, 'Blessed are the peacemakers' (Matt.5.9). Then the utopian vision will finally become truth: 'It shall come to pass in the latter days... that they shall beat their swords into ploughshares and their spears into pruning hooks; nation shall not lift up sword against nation, neither shall they learn war any more. O house of Jacob, come, let us walk in the light of the Lord' (Isa.2.2-4).

Dealing with God brings peace among men and women: this is a basic experience of the Bible. Jesus has removed the wall between the peoples, between 'Jew' and 'Gentile', and so has made access to the Father for all (Eph.2.14-18).

In the Hebrew root of the word *shalom*, peace, there is a reference to justice, to doing right and 'satisfaction': 'the work of justice is peace' (Isa.32.17), and therefore 'righteousness and peace kiss one another' (Ps.85.11). What does that mean?

The story of 'Adam who sinned in paradise' does not relate to a historical 'first man' on whom – with a reference to the excuse of 'original sin' – we can, thank goodness, foist off all doom and disorder in our history. The one who is meant is Everyman: everyone, you and I, all of us who share in this human history. It is to us, here and now, that the question after the Fall is addressed: 'Adam, where are you' (Gen.3.9). In our human history there is in fact war, feuding and dispute, battles (physical or moral) which are repeated in endless variations on a larger or smaller scale, horrifically grotesque and diminutively venomous, above all in smaller communities.

Are we still people of peace as God had intended at creation? We no longer know what it means to be able to be a human being, a person, and that above all before the face of the Lord. We human beings can certainly do a great deal: we have even widened the sphere of our world, into the stratosphere. So now we can also wage war in 'star wars' dimensions. But what we cannot do is to live together as human beings (with various differences), live together in an ordinary way. We hide behind customs and principles, behind views of life and even... religions. Here it is always *the other person* who is wrong! And so we keep away from the other person, inwardly uncertain and protecting our inner selves against the other. As we do that we are hardly aware that we are also hiding ourselves *from God*: 'Adam, where are you?' (Gen.3.9). We think: 'Adam – that's the other person, not me.'

'*You are not a God of confusion, but of peace*' (I Cor.14.33). From his creation onwards, God fights against chaos, the beast Leviathan: in nature, in the human heart, in human society. The Jewish tradition and also the Christian Bible call this fight 'creation'. Given the course of our human history, which even in its pristine youth began 'prototypically' with the disorder between the first two brothers and the chaos of the murder of Cain, peace constantly has to do with abolishing what is not peace, with 'making good', regulating or putting it in order: one must *make peace*. We must be concerned for peace. Peace, the Bible repeats, must be 'sought for'. It does not fall into our laps as a gift; peace must be done and made by human beings. It is there that the grace of God lies. Peace is a manifestation of God's grace seized by men and women – the worldly manifestation of human 'walking in the light of God'. The kingdom of God is the presence of God among men and women, affirmed or made welcome, active and encouraging, a presence which is made concrete above all in just and peaceful relations among individuals and peoples. And then it becomes evident that there can be peace only if the relationships between poor and rich countries are put right, thanks to the initiative of the rich or, if that does not happen, on the basis of the resistance of the poor. The letters of John say bluntly that anyone who says he or she loves God, but has no concern for a brother or sister, a fellow human being, is a liar. In modern circumstances this insight into the gospel includes a political commitment (from anyone who is called Christian) to a more just economic world system. We are liberated for brotherly and sisterly love. Peace is the visible manifestation of the state of redemption, the social dimension of a religious liberation. Peace means: 'It's going well.' Hence what people wish one another, *shalom* or *salaam*, i.e. in Hebrew and Arabic: 'May it go well for you', or 'All the best'! In Christian writings we read: 'May the God of peace... establish you in all good things' (Heb.13.20). Biblically that is a tautology, but for non-religious ears it is a necessary and urgent admonition, which they can also appreciate fully in humanist terms.

II. And yet: peacemakers polarize and bring division into the community

So far we have heard only about the biblical 'God of peace'. But this same Christian foundation document says with equal verve: 'Do not think that I have come to bring peace on earth; I have not come to bring peace, but a sword. For I have come to set a man against his father, and a daughter against her mother, and a daughter-in-law against her mother-in-law; and a man's foes will be those of his own household' (Matt.10.34-36).

There is clearly mention here of the essentially 'polarizing effect' of the appearance of all peacemakers, as also of peace movements within the church or between the churches. In other words: biblically speaking, polarization in the churches is anything but a bad word!

Rather, it is a gospel command. Anyone who unmasks human beings and society, as Jesus did, is regarded on the rebound by the society which is unmasked as a scapegoat, and ultimately done away with. In a famous book, R.Girard has analysed how any society which keeps itself in being by (constantly disguised) violence brings about psychological and social division, 'demonic possession' in society – which varies depending on the nature of the culture. So Jesus' time was full of demonic tormentors, of demonic possession; full of devils who sowed permanent anxiety among people living in a world of tyrants and idols. But where Jesus appeared, these tormentors disappeared and people felt free; all possession disappeared. Jesus' appearance was an unmasking of the hidden violence of the society of the time. The society did not tolerate this unmasking and was to take vengeance on him, as in fact happened. That is how the human scapegoat mechanism works.

Jesus – Martin Luther King, Bishop Oscar Romero and many others, all great pioneers in the order of peacemakers – indeed had a polarizing effect. So they were removed, 'censored', buried in the deliberate absence of the papal nuncio. In this ideology it is always already 'the other person' who polarizes. In the New Testament, as witnessed by the account of Jesus' polarizing influence on the specific society of his time according to the Gospel of Matthew, it is precisely the true peacebringers, like Jesus, who bring division to the so-called 'happy few'. This person is not at all concerned about the happy gospel of peace. A society which relies on concealed violence does not want to know anything about any unmasking of that violence. People disappear from it 'without a sound'. The tyrants wash their hands, as did the pawn of the Roman occupation of the time, Pontius Pilate: 'I find no guilt in this man': that is the slogan of any violent system.

There is no alternative: making peace brings polarization, 'the sword of division', everywhere: into churches, monasteries and families. Polarization of the kind that Jesus brought – 'the sword' or 'division' – may not have a name *in the church*. In the churches, polarization is a dirty word. But this word originally had a Christian, gospel name. It is precisely as a peacemaker, a manifestation of the peace of God, that Jesus brought the division of the spirits – not peace as the world gives it (John 14.27).

IV · Following Jesus: Active Pioneers and Those who Cross Borders

25

Domingo de Guzmán

Founder of the movement of 'the Dominican family'

At the word of welcome

'Think of the rock from which you are hewn' (from the ancient Constitutions of the Order of Preachers)

Let me first wish you all joy on this high feast of Dominic, which we may gladly and thankfully celebrate together.

As the Gospel reading I chose Matthew, because this was Dominic's favourite Gospel: he himself wanted his followers to know it off by heart. And from this Gospel I chose the story of someone who built a house on the rock (Matt.7.24-29), because Dominic, an almost unparalleled architect, indeed built his house, the Dominican community, on a rock.

Homily

In the south of France, in Vence, in a quite beautiful chapel of Dominican sisters, last year on Maundy Thursday I saw the famous Matisse pictures. On the wall of this simple chapel Dominic was depicted in a few strokes, but you could not say that the portrait was 'abstract'; it had just a few very evocative contours: very concrete and at the same time incomplete, figuratively abstract. If you look closer, you are impelled to fill in this sketch of Dominic yourself and yet you feel that your own interpretation is under the spell and the norm of this drawing. With gentle pressure the drawing itself indicates the direction of your colouring of it, while you yourself need not give up your own Dominican experience, from which you fill it in.

I thought: that *is* a full-length portrait of Dominic. Dominic was himself and granted others *their* space and freedom. We do not have a Hymn to the Sun from him, as we do from Francis of Assisi; nor even a Rule, like those of Benedict and Francis; we do not have a single writing from him, a single document in his own hand – which is also typical of Jesus of Nazareth. But we trace his spirit, we hear his 'logia' or sayings, and even his very own words, in some texts from the Fourth Lateran Council of 1215, very clearly in the first constitutions of the order, and finally above all in his living heritage: the Dominican movement. The French Larousse Encyclopedia, which is not a specifically Catholic work, calls Dominic the first 'minister of education' in Europe and another non-Christian historian calls him the first democrat in the church system.

It was on the initiative of Dominic that the Master General of the Order was not called abbot, prelate or any such title, but constitutional master, a leader who has no legislative power, but only executive power in respect of everything that the brethren of the annual General Chapter had laid down as guidance each year. It was also an extremely distinctive decision of Dominic to abolish the law then applying in all religious orders which made the Rule and Constitution obligatory on pain of sin so as to encourage the brothers and sisters. One has to be a religious from the heart, not under the threat of sin. The third Master General, Humbertus Romanus (II,46), relates that he had heard Dominic say through others: 'If anyone of our brothers (or sisters) thinks that the monastic rule is obligatory on pain of sin, then I will run round all the monasteries with a sharp knife to carve out every rule of the Order.'

Dominic has always seemed to me to be someone who is *par excellence* 'inwardly free', without complexes, liberated from concern for his own identity and therefore sovereign himself. He was an eminent administrator who, wary of all complicated legislation, simply gave his followers some rules of thumb, defined the direction and within that left space for others. As a personality Dominic was a kind of harmony of contrasts. On the one hand he was notable for an incredible lack of concern, in the sense of an almost audacious trust in God. The first Dominicans formed a happy community in the monastery of Saint-Romains, but Dominic abolished this monastery and scattered the members, apart from a few inhabitants, two by two round the world: to Paris and Spain, to Rome and Bologna. For a new religious foundation this seems to be one of Dominic's most reckless decisions. Moreover he was assaulted with doubts and advice from powerful sympathizers: Count Simon de Montfort, the Bishop of Toulouse, the Archbishop of Narbonne and many others urged Dominic not to do this. But Dominic's answer was brief but friendly: 'Don't contradict me, I'm well aware of what I'm doing.' History proved him right.

Moreover the same untroubled Dominic was an acute and purposeful organizer and strategist: he was as watchful as a fox, on his guard at every step. He calculates and calculates again, knows how to influence people for his apostolic projects, also under the impact of his human charm and natural authority. Sister Cecilia seems to have observed him closely. She testifies of Dominic: 'He was small in stature, rather slight in build, with a somewhat ruddy face, rather red hair and beard, attractive eyes. On his face, above all between eyes and eyebrows, there was a glance which cast a spell on many. He was always cheerful and alert, except when confronted with someone else's suffering. He had very long hands and a very resonant voice. Even when he grew older, he was not bald, but he had a short crop of light-grey hair' (Cecilia, ch.XV, p.30). So a woman can tell you something more about the outward aspect of a male saint.

Through cunning politics Dominic assured himself of the friendship of popes and other church and political authorities for his mission and apostolate. So he mobilized both the Fourth Lateran Council and the authority of the Pope for his project of 'the Dominican preaching'. Already through his financial administration, at least in the first period of the rise of the Order, he was one of the most stringent economists that the Order ever had. Many historians have been amazed at the way in which he acquires foundations and income; holds on to and expands, secures, leases out and develops what he has acquired; and does all this to free the brethren for study and above all for preaching the gospel. He would go back on that later. As he became older, Dominic made his views more radical and he then compelled all Dominican priories to cede all the property and collective possessions that they had gained, apart from humble dwellings with a small garden round them, to the Cistercian monks. In place of security of existence for the benefit of preaching, from now on Dominic wanted insecurity of existence out of solidarity with the poor and for the sake of the credibility of the preaching. That was the consequence of his acquaintance with Italian cities. In contrast to Spain and the cities in the south of France, Dominic now got to know the rich cities in Italy. He saw the greed and avarice in the cities which led to the building of rich palaces, but also to the impoverishment of many others which increased as a result.

Historical documents relate how Dominic's more radical approach by siding with the poor made many brothers leave the Order after the first General Chapter of Bologna in 1220. Dominic was resolutely opposed to the building of so many great priories because of the mass arrival of novices, and they remained incomplete until his death. Dominic was anything but a contemplative dreamer; he was God's fox, for God was the heart and soul of all that he did, and of his clear insight into what was going on in the church and the world. Although in my opinion (historians argue over this) he was not in agreement with the war which Count de Montfort waged against the Albigensians, he nevertheless calculated the fluctuating chances of this army in order to be able to exert skilful apostolic influence on the changing situation. Dominic built his house, his Dominican family, on a rock; he did this as an architect who calculates all the vicissitudes and takes them into account beforehand. Our first constitutions admonish us: 'Think of the rock from which you are hewn.'

Dominic was a charismatic, but with a very rational attitude, and I think that this combination was his success. Again there is a harmony of contradictions: evangelical sagacity coupled with a crystal-clear rationality. His rapture of spirit, his thoughtful practical wisdom, his well-known affable serenity: all this was paradoxically enough the work and the attitude of one prone to stomach ulcers who consequently had severe migraine, from which according to Jordan of Saxony he probably died. Psychologists assert that instability and moodiness, disquiet and lack of peace, chagrin, are all part of the psychology of those with stomach trouble and migraines. Jordan of Saxony, Dominic's friend and brilliant successor, nevertheless says of Dominic: 'The balance of his humour was remarkable.'

I could apply to Dominic what has been said of the apostle Paul in a way which is true to life but somewhat poetical: 'I am the Lord's singing bird. I build my nest in the mountain of my contemplation of God and I flop down there when I see a soul, as though Almighty God cast me down. I have long wished to ascend to the eternal tent on the heavenly plain. And hardly have I got up to the area of my desire above temple and obelisk than in the rarefied light such sorrow seizes hold of me that, heavy with mercy and compassion, I descend below again, and each time I there get a passionate love and hope of again becoming all to all' (here I am quoting from memory Fr Molenaer's, *In a Cool Shadow: Saint Paul* [*In koele schaduw: Sint Paulus*]. That is also a complete portrait of Dominic. They are the real saints; they no longer know whom they love best, God or human beings, because they can no longer distinguish between the two, so much are they 'of God', who is also a *God of men and women*.

Dominic was a man with a fine sense of the essentials in the great Christian tradition of experience, the essentials of the apostolic movement around the preaching brother Jesus of Nazareth. He was also a man with a fine sense of all the contemporary developments in the Middle Ages, in a period in which the old feudal system still predominated but was gradually being broken up by the rise of the free cities with their autonomous trades of free citizens. For the social and church system of the time, and also for many older religious orders, all this new development was 'of the devil', above all because in it a degree of emancipation of the laity was coming about which was furthered by the new techniques. People are often afraid of new developments; at that time for many people technology was a black and magic art, and cultural developments were disturbing the naive faith of some people. However, Dominic saw in this new social constellation a possibility of proclaiming the gospel in a new way: no longer for the benefit of a small élite but at least for a greater number, even if these were still primarily limited to the cities. Dominic, too, is a child of his time.

Judged by the ups and downs in our Dominican history, Dominicans, like Dominic, seem only to be at their best when a particular dominant culture is in process of disappearing and a new culture is making progress but is not yet dominant. Outside periods of crisis Dominicans seem regularly to go to sleep and rather to endorse uncritically the prevalent culture, even giving it theological justification. In this respect too we were often great teachers, and alas even grand inquisitors. Like Dominic, Dominicans only become more awake, alert and evangelical when something in the world is in process of springing up or bursting out and new signs of hope and freedom are announcing themselves on the horizon of society and culture. There are in fact people who are at their best in times of crisis and opposition; perhaps we are people of that ilk. But the presupposition for that must be that there is contemplation among us. Originally 'contemplation' means the opening up of land before a temple: a convenient place where it is good to sit and contemplate everything in tranquillity. So Dominic was a man of contemplation. And therefore legend could and might say that he spoke only to God or about God and human salvation, for that was the place from which he contemplated everything.

For Dominic this resting place for contemplation was no longer the temple nor even the monastery or the priory but the gospel of Jesus confessed as the Christ, the one who proclaimed the kingdom of God as good news for men and women: *to have the right to be there as a human being*. For Dominic, too, it was the case that only a God of life, not a God of life and death; only a living God, a God of the living and the dead who still know a future in him, can be worshipped, adored and celebrated by men and women: not a God who belittles or hurts human beings or humiliates them and denies them their joys. The whole of the life of Dominic was a paean of praise, a toast to God. That is where the secret of his pastoral feud with the Cathari and Albigensians lies, since he accuses them of having a twofold God, a God who humiliates and a God who raises up. For our doom-laden time, for people who no longer have any hope, Dominic remains a shining example of hope. Let us hope that this is so above all for our Dominican communities in a period of crisis for their existence. From this hope believers can still arise, believers like Dominic, Albertus Magnus, Thomas Aquinas, Bartolomeo de las Casas, Eckart and Henricus Suso, Catharine of Siena and Rosa of Lima, Martinus Porres, Lacordaire and Chenu, and so many others who have handed down to our day the torch of Dominic. Now this torch has been given into our hands. The critical question is: what do *we* do with it? That is the urgent message of Dominic for today.

At the prayers

Our Lord God

1. One of the earliest instructions for Dominican novices reads: 'Let it be clear to all who hear you that you are an authentic preaching brother: let it be given to them to be able to say, "Truly you are one of them: your manner of speaking betrays you."' We pray that we may perform our service of proclamation and reconciliation, and also do the work of truth and justice as Dominic would do it, not as wiseacres or sounding cymbals, but with understanding, with heart and warmth, so that we too no longer know whom we love the most: God or humankind. Let us pray.

2. We also pray for all men and women who work with us in greater or lesser union: for all who entrust themselves to the care of Dominican brothers or sisters; also for our sick brothers and sisters, on their sick-beds or elsewhere, who cannot join in this festival of Dominic; and for the religious of other orders and congregations, those who are at present experiencing the same problems as we are. Let us pray.

3. Finally we pray for wisdom for our church leaders, today above all for the Vatican Congregation of Religious, that it may not quench the fire of the Spirit where religious seek tentatively and experimentally for new forms of religious life and apostolic dedication. Let us pray.

Closing prayer of the eucharistic celebration

Let us pray

Lord our God, we thank you for the high feast of St Dominic and for the eucharist that we have been able to celebrate. We thank you for the gift which Dominic has been and still may be throughout our life. We ask you through Christ our Lord, forgive our failings. Amen.

26

Thomas Aquinas

Passion for truth as loving service to men and women

Rarely does human thought become religious worship, as it did in the case of the Dominican Thomas Aquinas, a theologian from the thirteenth century.

One Maundy Thursday, while his brethren were celebrating the Holy Week services and singing psalms in the choir, Thomas was in his cell writing an important work, a reply to a number of difficult pastoral questions which the Master General of his order had presented to him in view of his policy: we still have Thomas's booklet. Thomas justified this absence from the choir office, and in Holy Week, in a kind of artless self-defence – perhaps as a defence against some secret whispering in his religious community – as follows: 'Through study and writing I must compensate for the time that I cannot devote to singing psalms.' Thomas felt that his own life of study and writing books was the equivalent of what his brothers experienced as the choir office: an *opus divinum*, from of old the term for the liturgical worship of monks. For Thomas thinking is a form of praying, a distinctive kind of liturgical praise as a special form of 'being religious'. This attitude of Thomas's becomes clear from the plan of life which he himself explicitly formulated.

Writing in the first person by way of an exception, in his first great personal work, the *Summa contra Gentiles* – a kind of *vade mecum* for Dominican missionaries to non-Christian, Arabic Muslim countries – Thomas gave pointed expression (albeit in the form of a quotation) to the way in which he saw his own life's work. This is literally what he wrote: 'I clearly see as the predominant task of my life that I owe it to God to show and express him through all my words, thoughts and feelings' (Book 1, ch.2). Thomas experienced the general call to serve God in the service of one's fellow human beings as being realized for him in this form: to serve God by expressing him as God to fellow men and women; to let God be God by letting him speak to others through his own human words. The *raison d'être* of his life lies in this service to his fellow men and women, which consists *ex professo* of being occupied with God, in order then to let others share in these experiences and reflection on them. This is unmistakably also a specific form of what stands on the heraldic device of the Dominican order: '*Contemplata aliis tradere*', i.e. to share your own experiences of faith with others. This expression is, of course, taken by the Dominicans from an *opusculum* or short work by Thomas himself. For Thomas, being occupied in religious thought with God, human beings and the relationship between them is both a service to humankind and a distinctive kind of liturgical worship of God. Theological thought itself becomes both worship and apostolate. For Thomas, thought is the human material which he sanctifies as a Christian and dedicates to God and at the same time that with which he seeks to be of service to his fellow human beings.

In his *principium*, a mediaeval term for a university professor's inaugural lecture, given on the occasion of his promotion to the baccalaureate in the biblical sciences, Thomas speaks exclusively about his office as service of the truth. So I would want to see the life of Thomas as a 'priestly doctorate', as it were a priestly service of the word in well-thought-out form, expressed specifically for this time. As a theologian, Thomas stands with all his human capacity for analysis and power of thought in the Christian faith. He knows that theology is scientific reflection on what cannot be grasped scientifically, reflection on a datum which itself escapes all knowledge and can only be arrived at by those who in reflection are able to transcend thought in unconditional acceptance of God's self-evidence. However, for us, problematical people, this evidence is of course a mystery and can even become a problem. Moreover it is striking that this authentic theologian prayed to God every day that he should not lose his faith – that is what he says explicitly in a prayer of his which has been preserved.

For Thomas, 'not to lose faith' has a twofold significance, which has not lost its relevance even for us today. It means on the one hand that in our thought we may not abbreviate or undermine God's word of revelation; we may not cut it or mutilate it to the measure of our own understanding. But on the other hand it also means that we may not let the word of God turn into what in fact is human, time-conditioned presentation or thought: and so you may not impose on others a yoke that is not a liberating yoke of God, but the enslaving yoke of all-too-human theologians or prelates.

First of all: keeping faith intact. The liturgy of what Thomas calls 'the service of the truth' consists for him in the acceptance of the Other, God, as other, so that the datum of faith is not distorted into one's own image and making, but forms one's own thought and models it after the image that God has shown of himself through the history of salvation. Thomas does not want any blind spot in the eye as a result of which we stand selectively over against divine truths of salvation, according to the recipe of 'for each what he wants'. He does not want to obscure even one authentic facet of the reality of salvation: that would be being unfaithful to his priestly doctorate.

Secondly: not letting that pass for the Word of God which is not. For Thomas, to do that is just as much a form of loss of faith. Thomas had a remarkable sensitivity to this aspect of trust in the word of revelation which is expressed in two phrases which repeatedly occur in his works: *derisus infidelium* and *articulus fidei*. Here Thomas bears witness to the following. On the one hand, we may not express faith in such a way that we make this faith ridiculous to non-believers, for whom particular ideas of the faith inevitably seem naive, *passé* and ludicrous. In modern terms: Thomas points to the necessity of constantly reinterpreting or expounding faith, dogma, along the lines of what the dogma really means, and thus to the need for a demythologization of particular popular conceptions of faith. He requires this particularly as a form of trust in the authentic truth of faith.

Furthermore, we note Thomas's emphasis on the 'article of faith'. He constantly wants to discover whether or not we are dealing with mere 'church doctrine' or with an 'article of faith', i.e. with a religious truth which is one of the hinges or supports of the Christian gospel, without which the gospel is no longer a gospel of Jesus Christ. This points to Thomas's concern not to offend the human thought of others and to allow human thought in its own sphere to have complete freedom by making a more subtle distinction between God's word of revelation and the necessary but changing human expressions of it.

This double concern for correct or orthodox faith for himself and for others explains the fact that in his service of the truth Thomas is constantly fighting on two fronts at the same time.

On the one hand he is fighting against a variety of forms of integralism, which make a mockery of true confrontation. His library is filled with precisely those books which are suspect in current official theology: the latest studies of the pagan philosophers and of Jewish and Arabic thought, the modernism of the Middle Ages. Thomas is in search of truth wherever it is to be found, and thus already constructs a new Christian synthesis by which Christianity is fed for centuries after him.

'But there is also the second front on which Thomas worked and fought to preserve the faith. He argues against a variety of forms of brazen progressiveness, above all the audacity of Siger of Brabant and his followers. Because as a result of this his own life work in 'the service of the truth' had fallen under suspicion, this otherwise so serene and almost irritatingly balanced thinker suddenly became particularly biting. Words which are exceptional for Thomas like 'stupid', 'senseless' and 'terribly stupid' all stand exclusively in a context in which he is reacting against Siger of Brabant's so-called doctrine of double truth, which asserts that belief and talk can very well contradict one another and indeed may do so. This doctrine which Thomas fought against was also the reason why he was condemned on a number of points said to deviate from the teaching of the church, though this was after his death and only through a local bishop, the Bishop of Paris. This bishop, advised by anti-Thomistic elements at the Sorbonne of the time, did not see that Thomas, despite his stress on the autonomy of human reason in its own sphere, had taught quite differently from Siger of Brabant, whose teaching had then infected almost all the *facultas artium*, or faculty of philosophy. Later this same church canonized the condemned Thomas as a trustworthy church teacher, a secure guarantor of what was officially regarded as 'church doctrine'.

If we are ultimately in search of the mystery of the life of this man of study and prayer, we get the precise answer from Thomas himself. On his deathbed he cried out, '*Jesus... per cuius amore, Jesus, for love of whom* I have studied, *for love of whom* I have lain awake at night, *for love of whom* I have preached and given lectures...' In this dying cry Thomas, perhaps unintentionally, betrays the mystery of his life. No closet learning, no ambition or sheer intellectual curiosity explains this life of study. But loving service of a living Someone does; service of the man Jesus, whose *mysteria carnis* – as Thomas named those 'mysteries of living' brought about in Jesus' human and bodily way of life – he had described in many tractates and expounded as the summary and content of the church's faith that he confessed: that he is the 'Christ, the Son, our Lord'.

With his colleague in Paris, the Franciscan Bonaventure, Thomas was invited to the Council of Lyons as theological adviser to the bishops. On the journey to Lyons, the story has it, Thomas beseeched his God to let him die rather than reach the council with a cardinal's post as a possible reward. Thomas died on the way: in a Cistercian monastery where he spent the night on his journey to the council after a long day's travelling and had fallen sick. Dying, this man who was generally seen as an unworldly scholar asked the abbot for a tasty salt herring. As being a cardinal would have made it impossible for him to continue his life's plan of priestly learning, he might just as well die: then his task was finished. By leaving his great theological *Summa* incomplete, he would already impress on us in passing that the task of priestly learning always remains an incomplete life's work, that each generation must begin and continue again.

'Jesus, for the love of whom I studied.' To put it another way: because I loved. That is how Thomas might sum up his life on his death-bed: love in the form of the priestly or ministerial doctorate of the right word in search of the truth. To put it another way: love in the form of service of the truth which liberates men and women. That is why Thomas is a saint. And he is a special sort of saint. He is also a saint in his rational thinking. And our rational and technological age, above all our Western culture today, has special need of such saints.

27

John is his name

Twenty-five years after the death of John XXIII

There came a man, sent by God,
John was his name.
He came to bear witness, he had to bear witness to the light,
that all should believe through him.

These words, first used to describe John the Baptist, were not incorrectly applied to Pope John XXIII by the cardinal who during the second session of the Second Vatican Council gave the memorial address after his death.[1] In all simplicity, shortly after his election, Pope John had said of himself that he had heard that many people regarded him as a transitional pope.[2] I myself remember the general disappointment when Roncalli, at the age of seventy-seven, appeared in the loggia and took the name Pope John XXIII. The dismay was universal. He was in fact a transitional pope, but pope for a transition of the church to a new period; a period which may have been blocked again afterwards, but which in what it has brought about among Christians can no longer be held back or reversed.

I. Notes of memories

I want to make two points: *on the one hand*, barely three months after his election to be pope under the name of John, on 25 January 1959 Roncalli took the decision to summon an ecumenical council, to be preceded by a Synod of the Diocese of Rome, and he also planned a revision of the church *Codex*; *on the other hand*, two years later, during a retreat between 26 November and 2 December 1961, i.e. shortly before the first session of the council, he wrote in his *Spiritual Diary*: 'I notice in my body the beginning of some trouble which must be natural for an old man.'[3] Only a year later, on 23 September 1962, the whole world knew that the pope was threatened with an incurable disease. Moreover he himself was convinced that 'suffering and death' would be 'his very personal contribution' to the Council. Of the four sessions he was involved in only one. In the closing speech after the first session, moreover, he added the view that the Council could well end with the second session. This was somewhat naive, given the course of the first session. His simplicity was sometimes disarming.

In 1962 the expectations for the coming council were not particularly high. The Roman Synod, which had been a failure, was just over. In it the outlines prepared by Curia cardinals with their theologians had almost slavishly been approved by the fathers of the synod. John himself saw this Synod as a marvellous success. Some months before the Council began, moreover, there appeared from his own hand on 22 February 1962 an encyclical which at the same time was silenced throughout the Roman Catholic Church, *Veterum Sapientia*, about keeping Latin as the language of the church, including theology – the first thing that the Council would abolish, in the liturgy as well.

All kinds of legends and myths went the rounds about the person of Pope John and his relation to the council. But legends are sometimes the metaphysics of reality: legends do not just drop down from heaven; you must deserve them. It is well known from the first encyclical of Pius XI *Ubi arcano Dei* dated 23 December 1922 that this pope toyed with the idea of resuming the First Vatican Council which had been broken off by the war, but he did not dare to take a decision and wrote that he was 'waiting for a sign of God's will'.[4] But his pontificate in part coincided with the rise of Italian Fascism and the pope found that too unfavourable a time for a council. Subsequently, during the pontificate of Pius XII, Cardinal Ruffini, Archbishop of Palermo, suggested to this pope that he should convene a council. He wrote this himself on 4 November 1959 in the *Osservatore Romano* (two months before John XXIII made mention of a coming council): 'Twenty years ago (he was then Rector of the Lateran University) I ventured to talk to the pope about an ecumenical council.' The pope took note of this, and later talked with some prelates, but let things lie. Neither Pius XII nor the Curia had any intention at that time of shaking the firm position of the Roman Curia by calling in outsiders. Everything points to the fact that 'the Pentagon', as five cardinals were called (Cardinals Canali, Micara, Pizzardo, Mimmi and Ottaviani), were furious opponents of a council and did everything possible to stem the breakthrough to the world episcopate.

Pope John was perhaps familiar with the wish of Pius XI to resume Vatican I. But his idea had nothing to do with completing Vatican I. Moreover during the first months of his pontificate he got to know the tenacity of the Curia, but above all he knew what was going on in the churches in the world. For a number of years he had been Apostolic Visitor in Bulgaria, for some years after that he was

Apostolic Administrator of Turkey in Istanbul, and then he was papal nuncio for France in Paris. From 28 December 1952 he became patriarch of Venice: pastor of a diocese. He also knew that many French cardinals thought differently from the Roman Curia. He took the decision to summon a council without the Curia; he wanted to confront the Curia with a *fait accompli*. Therefore the bewilderment in the Roman Congregation seemed particularly great after the announcement.[5]

With a view to the coming council and to prepare for the opening speech, from 8 to 16 September 1962 John made a solitary retreat in St John before the Lateran Gate in Rome: there he regularly received only Fr Ciappi, a Dominican, who helped him with the Latin; now and then he saw his secretary Don Loris Capovilla; and every day for an hour his confessor, Mgr Cavagna. During this retreat he wanted to prepare himself for the council, but he already felt his illness seriously. Of this retreat he says that it did not become what he had hoped.[6]

Nevertheless, in his diary for those days he wrote down some very typical words. He says that God 'bestows great grace on anyone who does not exalt himself but receives these good inspiration and brings them to fruit in humility and trust.'[7] And he mentions two of these graces: 1. that the papacy had fallen to his lot when he had not wanted it and during the conclave had done everything possible to escape the notice of the cardinals; and 2. 'making use of a couple of simple ideas which could be carried out immediately', which was also decisive for the future.[8] He added to this that in the first conversation that he had with the Secretary of State on 20 January 1959 about the simple ideas that were easy to carry out 'without having thought of them beforehand', these thoughts related to the Ecumenical Council, the Diocesan Synod of Rome and the revision of the church law book, and 'to be honest, that went against my own assumptions and expectations':[9] 'I was the first to be amazed at my proposal, since no one had ever given me an idea of it.' He repeatedly came back to this sudden inspiration: 'An inspiration from the Most High.'[10] 'The idea of an ecumenical council was not the ripe fruit of long-drawn-out deliberations, but occurred to us like the amazing blossoming of an unexpected spring.'[11] It was 'the consequence of a spontaneous idea, which we felt in the simplicity of our heart as an unforeseen and unexpected shock'.[12]

I see it like this: (apart from protecting himself diplomatically against his own Curia, which he did not consult) Pope John must have toyed with the idea of a general council for a while from the time he was elected pope, knowing that above all such a council could loosen up a good deal in the church. There is something experimental about any council: you never know what will come out of it. And secondly, John must indeed have experienced the free *decision* which he suddenly took in solitude, to risk the council, as an unexpected grace. In the apostolic constitution *Humanae Salutis* of 25 December 1961 in which he summoned the council for 1962, he says that 'the Lord calls on us to learn to see "the signs of the times" (Matt.16.4). If we do that, we shall note, doubtless in the midst of so many dark clouds, numerous pointers which bring to the church and humankind the harbingers of a better time.'[13] He remained convinced that at least his solitary decision to summon a council had been a kind of divine inspiration. No longer in a private diary but in this same apostolic constitution *Humanae salutis* he says: 'As it were giving heed to an inner voice as a result of a supernatural inspiration we have therefore thought that the time is ripe to give the Catholic Church and the whole human family a new Ecumenical Council.'[14] His own doubt related to the question whether the time was indeed ripe for this.

Even for Pope John, initially what he envisaged for his council was still vague. However, the plan gradually began to take shape. In the first announcement during a solemn ceremony in the Basilica of St Paul's outside the Walls on 25 January 1959 he identified the aim of the council, very generally, as being twofold: 1. 'the illumination, renewal and joy of the whole Christian people', and 2. 'a sign of challenge to separated churches to seek unity'.[15] John also used the formula 'illumination and renewal of the whole Christian people' barely a month after his election as pope, in his Christmas message[16] of 1958, and in a conversation with the Latin American episcopate he stressed close collaboration between pope and episcopate: no one can solve problems on his own.[17] The second aspect, namely the stress on the ecumene, is certainly not strange given his stay in the Balkans, in Turkey and for a time in the Lebanon. On 25 March 1960 John agreed to a suggestion which one of the bishops had sent to Rome for the preparation of the council. He set up the Secretariat for Unity, of which Cardinal Bea was given the direction. But this first 'inner-church' and 'ecumenical' aim was gradually extended, to the world.

In the opening speech of the council, *Gaudet mater ecclesiae*, the pope made an unusually sharp plea to all the prophets of doom. What he actually said was: 'In modern times they can only see downfall and disaster; they are accustomed to saying that our time, in comparison with former ages, is steadily getting worse; they act as if they have learned nothing from history, though history is the teacher of life; they behave as if in the time of former councils everything was going triumphantly for Christian doctrine, Christian life and the legitimate freedom of the church. However, We are of the view that in all this We are not in agreement with these prophets of doom.'[18] For this man, Pope John, prophecies of doom were the fruits of anxiety. And then Pope John spoke the memorable words which afterwards continued to inspire many of the fathers of the council: 'I would rather,' he said, 'recognize the hidden guidance of divine providence in the present course of events.' That this was said after all the popes of modern times – up to and including John's predecessor, Pius XII – had condemned all the achievements of modernity as being of the devil, was in the council already the implicit beginning of internal tension between a 'majority' and a 'minority'.

The paradoxical situation of the time was that at the beginning of the council no one knew how big the majority was or how small the minority was and of whom these consisted. Were the majority 'conservative' or would they go in an 'open' direction? No one could give an answer at the time which was based on firm facts. There was hope – here and there even aggressive hope – of a new future for the church, but no certainty. The participants still lived and thought under the pressure of the *status quo* of the traditional 'curial majority', although at the time many people already knew that bishops from many backgrounds had complained against this curial status. At the beginning of the council the balance between the parties was anything but clear and simple. Many bishops wished that everything was still 'open', but nevertheless no one knew at the time. They feared the contrary.

In the opening speech which I have already quoted, John went on to clarify what he had in mind for the council: the sacred heritage of Christian teaching must be preserved and proclaimed in an effective way. He said that it was a matter of our duties as citizens of both this earth and heaven; but in addition, in handing on the store of truth 'account has to be taken of this time, of different circumstances and new norms of life', which also opened up new ways for the Catholic apostolate: this was the so-called *aggiornamento* of Pope John. In a simple way, but one which opens up a different perspective from what we had seen under the pontificate of Pius XII, in the same opening speech John drew a distinction between 'the substance of faith' and 'the way in which these truths are formulated, preserving the same meaning'. He laid stress here on the the fact that the teaching office in the church has a pastoral character. And in challenging notorious errors he said that he would prefer to use 'the healing means of mercy' rather than 'the weapons of strictness'. This rarely heard tone, at least from the lips of a pope, was an enormous encouragement to many bishops who wanted to make something concrete out of the council for the salvation of living men and women. Perhaps it was in his capacity as a historian that Pope John could say in this same opening speech: 'We have learned that violence against others, the power of weapons and political domination, are in no way sufficient to produce a happy solution to the very serious problems which trouble people.'

In his Apostolic Admonition *Sacrae Laudis* of 6 January 1962 he compared the coming council to the feast of Epiphany: guided by the star of Christ all bishops from all over the world would come to Rome like the 'wise men from the East'. The Second Vatican Council is certainly Pope John's council, but (as John wanted) it was the world episcopate that would have to make out of it what could be made. It is striking how all the speeches of this pope (who already knew that his days were numbered) in connection with the coming council are full of words of happiness: 'Everything tuned to joy,' he repeated in all his speeches. From what he perceived of the reaction of bishops to his initiative for a coming council, to an increasing degree he began to expect more of the council, as it were against his own original expectations.

On 17 May 1959 he set up the *Commissio Ante-Praeparatoria*. On 5 June 1959 ten auxiliary commissions and three secretariats were appointed. On 12 June 1961 the Central Preparatory Commission was set up under papal direction. In his *Diary* John wrote during a retreat from 26 November to 2 December 1961: 'A great deal of my daily work is in the preparation for the approaching Second Ecumenical Council (sic!).'[19] For he had once said with a laugh during the council, 'When it comes to the council we are all novices.' Neither the pope nor any bishops with their advisers had ever had any experience of a council. And none of us who were able to take part in the council could have thought that this period of the council would have been the most interesting time of our lives, as many conceded afterwards.

But the high point (though experienced by some as the nadir) of the breakthrough of the open majority in the council was 21 November 1962. An aula vote on 20 November had to decide whether the outlines (the so-called schemata) worked out above all by Curia cardinals and Curia theologians were to remain the basis for the council, though all kinds of amendments could be made to them, or whether after the considerable amount of criticism which had been expressed in the aula these preliminary drafts could be scrapped so that new commissions with a different orientation could write completely new provisional drafts. This was the most critical moment of the whole of the Second Vatican Council. In legal terms the situation was that the schemata prepared by the Curia were *in possessione*; in other words, only a two-thirds majority of all valid votes could consign these schemata to the wastepaper basket. The result caused utter dismay among the 'open bishops': fifty votes short of the two-thirds majority. This was a jubilant triumph for the curial 'minority' among the bishops, even though they had only one third of the votes.

But what no one had expected, and the next day came like a flash of Pentecost into the aula, was that, after a conversation with the 'Praesidentia' of the council, Pope John had decided that despite this shortfall of fifty votes the 'open majority' of the world episcopate formed the moral majority and that the new schemata should be rewritten in the direction which the criticism had indicated. Sensitive to freedom of opinion, John simply asked that the two trends should carry on a conversation in a mixed commission about the themes which had not been sufficiently established by the pre-conciliar commissions in a real dialogue. It was a happy day for many fathers of the council; by this decision, they felt, the pope had opened the way to a council that could become what in fact it did become. In this sense, too, Vatican II is *his* council: Pope John's council. Without this fundamental decision by the pope (in fact, from a purely legal point of view, in conflict with the conciliar 'regolamento' that he himself had approved) the council would have take a very different course.

II. More than twenty years later

Only now, twenty years after the council, after and in the time from 1967 up to and including 1988, which some have already called 'the time of the anti-council', can we properly measure and analyse the real significance of Pope John for the Second Vatican Council.

With all his brilliance, after the council Chenu called Vatican II the end of the Constantinian period in the church and the victory over the Tridentine and post-Tridentine period. I too am convinced that Pope John saw, more out of intuition than clear calculation, that the church system as it had hardened under the tradition of the Pius popes could no longer have any future. He saw that it had been a church which condemned all the new and good things which came to life outside the church and glorified itself within the horizon of an imperialistic view of truth as the one and only source of truth. The crisis of the 1970s, of which some think that the council was the cause, was already latently in the making before the council. The identification of the priest with a sacral *persona*, the identification of sacramental penitence with auricular confession, the identification of the liturgy with priestly presidency – to mention only a few symptoms – were already in very real crisis before the council, even if many people had not yet realized the fact. There were many signs of a world-wide discontent with the church. Moreover already beforehand Pope Pius XII, too, had perceived that discontent. But his diagnosis was that it was a sickness which had to be challenged.

By contrast, in his opening speech of the council Pope John said that it was a sign of the times – looking back, we can say that it was high time to close the Constantinian, post-Tridentine period and open a new future for the church. Of course Roncalli did not put it in these words, but in fact in contrast to the pessimistic encyclicals of Pius XII he had learned from the 'encyclicals' of Cardinal Suhard of Paris, where he was nuncio, which were famous at the time, that the *status quo* of the church was preventing any *aggiornamento* even in terms of the gospel.

Objectively speaking, Vatican II is a break with this pre-Vatican, ossified church, a break involving all that the church had then condemned, namely freedom of conscience, freedom of religion, ecumenical openness, democracy and toleration. Vatican II is the break with a centuries-long post-Tridentine church mentality. During the council I heard someone (his name now escapes me) say, with my approval, 'This is the end of mediaeval Augustinianism' (this last applied in my view above all before the pastoral constitution *Gaudium et Spes*, which was already said at the time by the theologian Ratzinger to be far too optimistic).

This epoch-making shift in our church history was, with hindsight, the deepest significance of Vatican II and moreover of Pope John, although he had only one session with the Council. But this was the decisive session. Therefore the view of some who assert that Vatican II is the completion of Vatican I is historically an incorrect estimation of Pope John's council. What the post-conciliar 'anti-council' (in the sense of mentality) is really doing (and the arch-conservative Mgr Marcel Lefebvre is still the most consistent exponent of this) is to entrench itself behind a late-Tridentine traditionalism.[20] What Lefebvre is doing honestly and consistently, others are doing in a clandestine way: they differ from Lefebvre only in tolerating no criticism of John-Paul II. Yet in their undermining of the council they are doing precisely what Lefebvre is doing, and the Curia now seems ready to capitulate to his retrospective anathema. That would be the burial of the council! In that case 'papalism' is involved, not 'the council', and in the meantime one can and evidently may completely deny its spirit, even with the curial blessing of Rome.

III. Vatican II and historical irony

But there is also a certain historical irony about Vatican II, though this is misused by traditionalists above all to attack the Vatican *Gaudium et Spes*, namely that in the period 1964-1965 there in fact was a breath of the optimism of the time after 'the cold war', in which figures like Kennedy, Kruschchev and Pope John XXIII dominated the world stage. But quite apart from the conservative misuse of this 'historical situatedness' of the council, one may not argue away the reality of this historical situation.

At all events, it is an undeniable fact that only after this council did the call come in our world for more democratization of all official institutions, along with the student unrest; only then did great world problems with deeply human resonance come to general public attention: nuclear energy, nuclear weapons, the pollution of the environment, the exhaustion of our natural resources, the oil crisis and the shift of the East-West conflict to the north-south conflict. The Eurocentric place of the central European churches was weakened and we Europeans became more than ever aware of our regional and therefore one-sided self-understanding.

Moreover the 1970s were the years of the great alarm about our prosperity. This led to despair, helplessness and anxiety: people saw the fragility of the political and economic world situation. Periods of crisis are often fruitful in radicalizing, conflicting trends: they attract polarization. Many people escaped in an apolitical way into 'contemplative' inwardness; others escaped into external wantonness, grim vandalism – often without soul and inwardness, without the will to make the humanity in ourselves and others survive.

The contrast with the 1960s, in which the council took place, could not be greater. At that time we lived in a world which had surmounted the chaos of the Second World War and which was becoming over-confident through economic progress and an international perspective on peace (even if that was ambiguous). We find something of the naive optimism of those days in the pastoral constitution *Gaudium et Spes*, in which the church had given conciliar definition to its own role and contribution in the great development of humankind on the way to universal prosperity and well-being. But since the 1970s we have been confronted with a very different picture of the world, and we have to be careful and economize.

So after the council there was a general change in the cultural and social climate, also as a result of economic circumstances. However, this council was nevertheless itself also a council of protest and opposition, albeit in a different situation: it was a reaction of the liberal church against the feudal and monarchical remains in the church of the nineteenth and twentieth centuries. Only in the Second Vatican Council were the great achievements of the French Revolution and of bourgeois liberation – tolerance, freedom of religion, freedom of conscience, ecumenical openness, no monarchical one-man government ('collegiality') and so on – officially approved by the Roman Catholic Church and, after a long dispute in the church specifically against these bourgeois values, introduced sympathetically into that church, precisely at the moment when the world was beginning as it were *en masse* to criticize the new slaveries which liberal bourgeoisie has produced in its own lands but above all in the Third World. This is the irony of the history of Vatican II: the phenomenon of the church often coming too late. All this at the same time hindered the implementation of the basic thrust of the council. New problems arose for the church even before people could pluck the fruits of this council – late, but full and ripe. Moreover some seized on these new problems to cast suspicion on the achievements of the council. Instead of turning bourgeois freedom (*my* freedom) into the priority of *the other person's* freedom and thus solidarity, the traditionalists of many shades want to go back to a pre-bourgeois, feudal or monarchistic one-man government.

The deepest intention of the 'episcopal collegiality' intended in Vatican II by the majority of the world episcopate (as collegial government of the church in contrast to an 'absolute monarchy') by a one-sided *nota praevia* dropped from outside the council (under the pressure of three 'papal theologians') during the pontificate of Paul VI. This weakening remains the baneful foundation of what one can call the present situation of 'the period of the post-Vatican anti-council'. Pope John would never have done anything like that!

With all this post-Vatican context, Vatican II has completely disappeared from sight as a point of reference for inspiration and orientation, above all for younger people. That is what I mean by the post-Vatican situation. The call for a 'conciliar process: justice and peace and the integrity of creation', a process which is finding an echo among Christians everywhere but which, while it could not be rejected by the Roman Curia with its cautious diffidence was not warmly welcomed (as being 'an initiative from outside'), has evidently replaced or taken over the inspiration of Vatican II. In this new situation we lack from the Roman Catholic side a reaction which, in the spirit of Pope John XXIII, is an adequate response to the initiative that has been announced.

For the moment the 'spirit of Vatican II' is indeed dead and gone in the official Roman Cathoic church. Nevertheless, this spirit lives on, faithful to the council, in the grassroots, among numerous believers, and there this spirit cannot be tamed. The Roman Catholic church embraces more than what is usually called the 'Roman Curia' under the leadership of the pope – with or without a *nota praevia*!

Notes

1. See John XXIII, *Geestelijk Dagboek en andere geestelijke geschriften*, Tielt and the Hague 1965, 521.
2. John XXIII, *Diary of a Soul*, London and New York 1965, 385.

3. Ibid., 387.
4. *Documentation Catholique* no.139, 1959.
5. See an article in *Informations Catholiques Internationales*, 15 October 1962, 73.
6. Ibid., 389-94.
7. Ibid., 393.
8. Ibid., 394.
9. Ibid., 394.
10. *Motu Proprio 'Superno Dei nutu'*, Pentecost 1960, see *Katholiek Archief* 14, 1959, 609.
11. Ibid.
12. *Exhortatio* to the clergy of Venice, 21 April 1959, see *Katholiek Archief* 145, 1959, 680.
13. Ibid., 494.
14. Ibid., 496.
15. *Katholiek Archief* 14, 1959, 371-76.
16. Christmas Message 1958, in *Katholiek Archief* 14, 1959, 52.
17. Address to CELAM, *Katholiek Archief* 14, 1959, 3.
18. *Archief der Kerken* 17, 1962, (979-88) 981.
19. *Diary of a Soul*, 386 (here the English translation does not reflect the original Italian).
20. See *Die Rezeption des Zweiten Vatikanischen Konzils*, ed. H.J.Pottmeyer, G.Alberigo and J.-P.Jossua, Düsseldorf 1987; in it Alberigo, 'Die Situation des Christentums nach Vaticanum II', 15-44; also E.Schillebeeckx, *Vatican II: The Real Achievement*, Geoffrey Chapman 1967 (US title: *The Real Achievement of Vatican II*, Herder and Herder 1967, Vol.2); Metropolitan Nikodim, *Johannes XXIII. Papst einer Kirche im Aufbruch* (translated from the Russian), Berlin 1984.

28

'Not that we lord it over your faith'

The Pope's visit to the Netherlands

When I think of the coming of the Pope to the Netherlands, a saying of the apostle Paul impresses itself on me, and so I want to take it as a guideline. It occurs in his second letter to the Christians of Corinth – in church affairs at that time a 'maverick' which was making things difficult for Paul: 'Not that we lord it over your faith, but we work with you for your joy' (II Cor.1.24).

If Pope John Paul II wants to come to the Netherlands, we do not require him to arrive in Amsterdam in Peter's fishing boat. We live in the 1980s. He may arrive in a plane and step out into a bullet-proof popemobile, and all this may cost something: that is real and normal. The important thing is the message that we shall hear, and its credibility.

What we expect from him as Christians is the gospel: a message of joy and hope. What he must come and do is look at people here, as God looks at all people, above all the least among them. Anyone who does that looks round, and up, to the living God. That contrasts to the possible coming of a lawgiver who would only present legal texts, would not see the good that there is here and would only want to point out our weak spots. There are weak spots among us, as there are elsewhere. He might well, as in the book of Revelation, praise and rebuke the angels of our dioceses, but in the sense that: 'I know your deeds' (Rev.3.8). But do you know our deeds? This presupposes good information (which even Paul sometimes lacked).

When I reflect on the papal visit, I do it from my special role as a theologian, and thus really as a simple Christian: as someone in other words who speaks of God in relation to people, not too early but also not too late, expressing God in the midst of the ups and downs of human life.

'The church' is in the religious service of real people. As the bearer of the keys the Pope should appear above all as a factor of unity, i.e. with a concern for both the unity and catholicity, i.e. the polycentric, cultural embedding, of the one gospel in the many different church provinces or local churches. Anyone who wants unity without pluriformity ultimately attacks unity. Anyone who advocates hit-or-miss pluralism without unity damages faith.

My concern is that the further we move away in history from the Second Vatican Council, the more some people begin to interpret unity as uniformity. They seem to want to go back to a monolithic church which must form a bulwark on the one hand against Communism and on the other hand against the Western liberal consumer society. I think that above all in the West, with its pluralist society, such an 'ideal' of a monolithic church is out of date and runs into a blind alley. And there is the danger that in that case people with that ideal before their eyes will begin to force the church in the direction of a ghetto church, a church of the little flock, the holy remnant. But though the church is 'not of this world', it is 'of men and women': men and women are the believing *subjects* of the church.

Moreover it is not just my impression but also that of many others that the manifold visits of the Pope implicitly bring with them an undervaluation of the local bishops and of what they think good in their situation for the believers who are entrusted to them. When one adds to that the way in which a growing number of bishops overestimate the role of the Pope in the life of the church, one can see that among believers the term 'the church' is increasingly identified with 'the Pope'.

It is depressing to have to note the fact, but the idea of collegiality which was fought for with holy zeal in Vatican II has in practice disappeared from the church since the year 1985. The more time goes on, many newly nominated bishops tend even to take on the voice of the Pope in that re-centralization process, in the sense that they become only the channel for what he proclaims or even says ordinarily, as a thinking person, at many audiences – without speaking their own words, without taking account of the specific pastoral problems of their cultural area: in that way the distinctive colour of their own church province threatens to be misunderstood. It even seems that some bishops do not regard their own church province with any warmth and can say nothing good of it.

If I quote Paul's saying, it is out of a deep concern that conceptions born and nurtured in the centre are being imposed compulsorily, even in detail, on the local churches, for which by virtue of their office the local bishops are primarily responsible. The Pope is *pope*, exercising the function of Peter, also for and in the Catholic Netherlands, but he is not a local bishop here. He is the last resort, the arbiter standing above the parties, in communion 'with the eleven'. I feel that a degree of anxiety, an uncertainty on the part of local bishops, is also at the root of this. They do indeed face great problems, but they foist these on the centre. Even the conferences of bishops, which were also meant to do pastoral justice to the local church in their own culture and to the specific problems of a country or region, are having a hard time. And people 'up there' tend to be pleased about this. Moreover we see increasingly that particular bishops are isolating themselves and are only maintaining a direct line with Rome and the lobbies there, from which they expect and hand down instructions. That breaks through both the 'soft' and the 'hard' ideas of collegiality of Vatican II, as they were called at the time in the corridors of the council: 'cheap', social solidarity, and 'ecclesial-collegial' solidarity, which is theologically to be taken seriously.

So in the centre there is also growing fear of local new insights and renewal movements, and opposition to experimentation, whether this is the indigenous liberation theology in South America, the liturgical movement in Africa or the emergence of male and female pastoral workers in the Netherlands. There is a vicious circle in on the one hand the claim of the central authority and on the other hand the way in which many bishops pander to this authority, sometimes even against their own conviction, as I have heard (worldwide) in confidence from some bishops.

Let me return to the text from Paul: 'We are not lord and master over your faith.' It may seem harsh to apply that saying literally, as a possibility, to the impending visit and preaching of the Pope. But today's preaching, as it comes to us from Rome and from local bishops, certainly also in the Netherlands, seems to be less about the needs of men and women – in search of belief – than untold repetition of what the pastoral authority did in former times and (often rightly) meant that it has to be done for the benefit of believers. But the ice-cold repetition goes on as if our 'present' is an abstraction, something that need not be taken into account.

However, one can also use dogmas as bricks to throw at people. In this way one shatters the broken reed. But according to Thomas, the wise man from Aquino, witness to a long tradition of experience, dogmas are hinges: the *cardines* on which everything relating to human salvation turns, and does so in such a way that men and women feel this mystery of life sharply in their own lives. Above all in the Netherlands, we see so much goodwill among men and women, so much warmth for the church, so much love for the gospel. Or is 'the dogmatic heart' of 'those in authority' so hardened that they do not even see the living reality of the gospel in the Netherlands any longer; alas cannot see it any longer (perhaps despite all good will)?

Any church province must listen to the Pope, certainly when he is addressing a particular church province directly *qua* pope. But the Pope must also listen to the church province: to the spirit which also blows there, in accordance with its own spiritual condition and not with authoritarian hierarchical approval. And if the local church says under the pressure of conscience that it is in fatal danger if authority speaks only in the language of rules and decretals, then the Pope should not only accept this cry, a people's *cri de coeur*, with good will, but should also reflect on the methods and strategies used in Rome.

May Pope and bishops not be those 'of little faith', who do not believe in their own church! They must have trust in the faith of a church province where the faith of our fathers and our mothers is preserved, and also the desire for an abiding bond with Rome. Great opportunities for the church for the benefit of men and women seem to be being missed by the reintroduction of what to many committed Catholics seems to be a pre-Vatican picture of the church. Or is true faith to be measured by the degree to which one is in tune with the angelic guardian? How am I to know?

'I come to increase your joy,' wrote Paul – generously – specifically to a community which had made things particularly difficult for him. Difficult churches are usually lively churches. The complaint of the 'angel of the church in Laodicea', 'I know your deeds, you are neither cold nor hot. *If only you were cold or hot!*' (Rev.3.15), certainly does not apply to the church province of the Netherlands. Here there is no fear of hot issues. Certainly mistakes will be made as a result. But in all their honest attempts believers, human beings, look for encouragement and endorsement, for the raising up of the broken reed; for blowing on the dimming flame. And as Catholics we may certainly expect from a Peter figure, called 'the Pope', 'the rock on which the church is built' (Matt.16.18-19), this gesture of raising up, not breaking, the already broken reed. The church is built upon him, along 'with the Eleven', the twelve foundation stones of which Revelation 21.14 speaks. 'To whom else should we go?', says Peter, the spokesman of the Twelve, to Jesus (John 6.68).

Without having any high expectations I just wish this: may this papal visit include the recognition of the questing faith that is found here in the Netherlands and throughout the Benelux countries. May it create space: a climate of justice, joy and peace for those who have been diminished and are kept diminished, but who as Christians stick out their neck, as Paul too dared to do.

Why he, Paul, and not us – in all humility but at the same time in Christian pride – also as people of the Netherlands?

29

'Where are the Eleven?'

In memory of Cardinal Alfrink

After his appointment as archbishop in 1955 Alfrink wrote in his first pastoral letter about his ministry: 'Not that we lord it over your faith, but we work with you for your joy' (II Cor.1.24). And that in fact was the way in which Cardinal Alfrink acted in the church. He was fashioned as 'Cardinal Alfrink' by his church province, just as he for his part also gave form to this local church. Seldom have I experienced in such a way the degree to which someone can be 'formed' and thus become 'great' through the particular form of a local church, while he in turn gave form to this church. Without being slack, but rather quite deliberately, Alfrink let the weeds grow with the wheat, and although he could also admonish, it was never 'as lord and master of our faith'. He also grew with the new ideas and new practices which were growing in the Catholic Netherlands at that time. He once said to me (in connection with his difficulties with the Vatican): 'To think that this is happening to me, when I am basically a conservative!', for that is what he was at heart.

He himself expressed his basic attitude like this: 'We have deliberately learned to understand giving leadership as the exercising of office in dialogue and we have sought to avoid the impression of wanting to cling to authoritarian action as was formerly practised and seemed natural,'[1] or again: 'We determine church government in our province together in divided and varied responsibility.'[2] 'We,' this expression was not a Byzantine, official church term for 'I' (= Cardinal Alfrink), but given the context of the Dutch Pastoral Council of the time meant: you (lay people, men and women, scholarly experts and theologians) – all those here present – along with 'us, bishops'. Alfrink never caused polarization among the people of God; he may have sometimes admonished his church province, but he never came down on it like a grand inquisitor on outsiders. Many people will remember his famous defence of the Dutch church province barely a stone's throw from the Vatican and in the presence of many bishops and cardinals. In my view this was one of the bravest actions of his time in office: to stand up for the community of God which had been entrusted to him. Is that not one of the main tasks of bishops down the ages? His watchword was to look after his people here, even when in his view they had gone too far.

Alfrink was not a 'man of little faith', not like an overseer who does not believe in his own church and prefers to give it a kick, becoming great by belittling others. For precisely that reason he had authority and there was no need for an 8 May movement. The whole of the people of God was, as always, in its ups and downs, one 8 May movement, unanimously and benevolently guided by the bishops and encouraged by Bishop Alfrink. At that time one could still feel every day the spirit of the Second Vatican Council: the Holy Spirit which blows where it wills and which had not been tamed and channelled into unhealthy ways. It was Alfrink who said: 'The last thing you can do is to wield the whip.' So he dared to speak of 'having the courage to take responsibility on yourself precisely by being permissive', 'so as not to tear up the wheat with the weeds'.[3] For the sake of this leadership in the light of the gospel he was sometimes maligned in an un-Christian and coarse way by inane people who were themselves inwardly uncertain and therefore leaned towards authoritarian rule from outside, above all in pamphlets by people who boasted of being 'the holy remnant' – a term against which Jesus of Nazareth, nevertheless 'the Christ', had prophetically protested in the Gospels.

But for Alfrink (as for us all) it was equally important 'to keep the integrity of the message of the Lord'.[4] Here, however, he preferred the pastoral method (concern for 'the human person') 'to an attitude of resolute determination which could bring with it the danger of oppression and threaten to drive a number of believers from the church',[5] as he wrote, defending himself and above all 'his church'. Alfrink had respect for the questing faith of many people. He gave encouragement and support; he raised up the broken reed and kindled the dimming flame. He was a church leader; not a prelate, but a leader at the right moment.

But one cannot force Alfrink one-sidedly into the role of someone who closely followed the movements of his church and knew how to delegate, someone who also trusted the faithful, even when he himself sometimes frowned on particular developments. In some cases he was even a step ahead of his church province. It remains to *his* credit that even before the Second Vatican Council he stressed episcopal collegiality or the collective episcopal guidance of the church, which he also wanted to see extended to a kind of permanent 'papal privy council'. During the council his watchword was 'Peter *with* the

Eleven'. He argued that the Vatican Curia must be merely the executive organ of this papal privy council.

Alfrink wanted to make both the church and, above all in his position as President of Pax Christi, the world 'a place fit to live in'. No less a figure than Mgr J.Bluyssen put it like this – in an allusion to the epitaph of the one Dutch pope, Adrian VI: 'But it matters a great deal at what point full justice is done to someone's questions – and I am thinking of the best, even the VIPs.'[6]

Alfrink was in fact an active source and at the same time a passive result of what had taken place in Dutch Catholic life between 1955 and 1976. Later – at some historical remove – historians will (and can) give a meaningful evaluation of this. Alfrink, though he had a sharp sense of history, contributed little or no information to this future historically correct judgment on the Dutch church province between 1955 and 1976. When I once asked him whether he would ever write his memoirs in connection with his contacts with Rome he said (really proudly): 'History will never repeat what Paul VI said to me in the difficult times of the final period of the Dutch Pastoral Council.' According to my personal notes I then observed: 'But Rome certainly has records and you don't, and that will give the Roman archives the edge for the historian.' He was somewhat taken aback (suddenly realizing that), but nevertheless he said (just as stubbornly): 'No one will hear anything about it *from me*.' And alas, I am convinced that he meant that seriously. After so many confrontations with the Curia he was anti-curial (not rationally, but rather 'emotionally'). The Rector of the Collegio Olandese in Rome had as it were to prod him repeatedly and almost plead with him to have more contact with the Vatican authorities.

Despite this anti-curial attitude of Alfrink's (or was it fear?) at the same time, up until the papal visit to the Netherlands and to the last day of his life, he was a model of papalism which in this context is to be understood as unconditional trust in the Pope, whoever that might be. For him, Rome was not the Vatican bastion, but Peter, though always Peter *with the Eleven*. I think (I do not know) that in the last years of his life, Cardinal Alfrink, perhaps bewildered and rather sad, will have thought: '*Where are the Eleven?*'

Notes

1. *Analecta* 43, 1970, 90-1.
2. Ibid., 91.
3. Ibid. 46, 1975, 20.
4. Ibid. 43, 1970, 95.
5. Ibid. 44, 1971, 32.
6. *Alfrink en de Kerk 1951-1976*, Baarn nd, 7.

V · In Jesus's Footsteps in the 1980s

30

The conciliar process

Justice, peace and the integrity of creation

Terms which are sometimes used almost as slogans in what people have begun to call 'the conciliar process of mutual obligation for justice, peace and the integrity of creation' of the World Council of Churches call for some sharpening and purging. The special number of the Dutch journal *Wending* has carried this out carefully and in so doing has done us all a good service.

The purging and sharpening of the use of terms like 'process', 'conciliar', 'conciliar process', 'justice', 'peace', 'integrity' – the wholeness, becoming whole, making whole of – in short, concern for the creation were extremely necessary, because here and there talk about the conciliar process had turned into the bandying of slogans.

However, some believers, both Catholic and Reformed, have another difficulty which is only mentioned in passing in that number. Many believers are hesitant about the way in which the church is beginning to concern itself so intensely with 'worldly problems': with injustice in the world, with structural poverty – one of the main reasons why there is no peace – with the death of the forests, the poisoning of all water, with political and social torture and murder, and so on. They are afraid that as a result the church is forgetting its real religious mission or pushing it into the background.

But in connection with the religious mission of the church and its proclamation of the gospel it is extremely important to see that the conflicts which dominate 'the world' can also be found at all levels in the churches. It has rightly been said that 'what divides the world also divides the church'. Therefore in my view the future of the churches lies in their active presence in the future of the world of human beings and in healing nature: men and women, society, history and nature must be saved. There is a positive, inner bond between commitment to the justice, peace and wholeness of creation on the one hand and the kingdom of God on the other, which already began with the covenant of creation. But human beings constantly fail and cause new disasters. The struggle for a more human, more just world for all men and women, and therefore in the first place for poor and oppressed people, offers the possibility of a true understanding of the gospel and thus of the inculturation of that gospel in a local culture.

The conflicts which are brought into being by our economic system and structural poverty also define the content of the Christian, gospel witness. In place of the former contrast between 'the light' of Christianity and 'the darkness' of the non-Christian religions, we are now aware of what the Bible calls 'this world', i.e. the good world of creation *in so far as* in it not only sinful personal actions are done but also 'sinful structures' are brought into being; these structures then cause even more injustice and disruption by their own relatively autonomous weight. Over against the world of disaster there stands the same good world of creation *in so far as* in it God brings about salvation and wellbeing, as part of religious salvation, in and through human action. The active presence of the churches at the forefront of these conflicts which divide the world and therefore also the church communities of faith is the primary missionary action of the church. The religious relationship of men and women to God is for believers the deepest reason for this dedication to humankind, its society and history, and to making a sullied nature whole. The covenant of creation obligates us to this.

Really the summons of the World Council of Churches calls on us to set in motion the 'conciliar process' in the churches in order to take seriously Jesus' message and praxis of the kingdom of God. The kingdom of God is the message, the vision, of a new world in which suffering is done away with, a world in which people are completely whole or made whole in a society in which justice and therefore peace prevail and in which there are no longer any master-servant relationships – and thus a quite different situation from that under Roman occupation at the time of Jesus: what went on then 'may not be so among you' (Luke 22.24-27; Mark 10.42-43; Matt.20.25-26). However, this new world, although transcendent and a pure gift of God, will not come about without the mediation of human action, to the finitude and human limitations of which God gives a new future beyond death.

That the healing activity of Jesus and all his actions freeing men and women from need and distress go with his messianic task is also shown by the fact that Jesus does not send out his disciples just with the task of handing on his message of the forgiveness of sins and eternal life, but also with the task of 'healing people' (Mark 3.14-16; 6.7ff.). Those who were able to experience in Jesus salvation from

God were also themselves called to follow in Jesus' footsteps, 'to go around doing good', even to a greater degree than Jesus did (John 14.12), in unconditional love for their fellow human beings as the specific form of the all-embracing love of God. Why should the church here be 'horizontalizing itself' to what is then termed 'pure humanism' – which is what some people accuse the churches of? For believers, is not 'healing' people a preliminary sign of the kingdom of God – the kingdom of God on the way?

Nevertheless, at the same time there is a basic experience here which believers and agnostics have in common and which may therefore be the foundation for a united praxis in solidarity. In this common task, undertaken on the basis of a variety of inspirations and orientations, but as a result of the same fundamental 'irritation' (or the opposition which lies in any experience of contrast: things cannot be like that!), the churches can also 'make an alliance' with non-Christians, try to commit one another to another practice which gives shape to more humanity, more justice in the world, in a world which needs to be healed. The gospel mission seeks a connection with those areas of the population where the call of humankind for freedom and human worth, justice and peace resounds loudly, for Christian hope and expectation for the future become concrete only if they become involved in the human tragedy of poverty, injustice and oppression. That was the distinctive perspective of Jesus' own mission: 'The good news is preached to the poor.'

The message of Jesus embraces the kingdom of God in all its height and depth, breadth and length, and not just the forgiveness of sins and eternal life. To bring the gospel to all who suffer in the world, not only by word but above all by action in solidarity, is the essence of Christianity. Therefore Christian mission also has to do with questions of justice and peace, of the division of material and spiritual goods, the distribution of work, more equitable trade relations and a fairer world economy, which also respects and honours nature. Precisely because these problems can only in fact be solved in a world alliance, the Christian mission in our time more than ever takes on a more concrete universal significance.

In the present socio-political and economic setting of structural injustice for the majority of people, the Christian gospel does not only or primarily 'universalize' caritative diaconia (which Mother Teresa practises so well), but above all political diaconia, which seeks to remove the causes of this structural poverty and in so doing recognizes the universality of human rights and human values. The transformation of the world into a higher humanity, into justice and peace, is an essential part of the universality of the Christian message, and this is *par excellence* a non-discriminatory universalism.

31

You and I have a right to be there

The first 8 May demonstration at the Malieveld, The Hague, 8 May 1985[1]

Introduction

All of us are here together not only to show the other face of 'our church' but also to celebrate it. Despite the unfavourableness of the moment, we oppose the prophets of doom who are increasing among us, the voices which tell us that what developed through experiments and explorations in the Netherlands and elsewhere since the Second Vatican Council should be done away with everywhere. The presupposition of this particular way of thinking is that the term church must be identified with the supreme authorities of the church. And what do we have here in this tent and outside it as a sign of the authority of powerless believers? Or do *we* not count? Do more than 100 Catholic organizations and many committed believers stand outside the breathing and sighing of the Spirit? More than 10,000 Christians present here!

A theologian tries to express what is alive in the communion of faith and to compare this critically with the already lengthy, seething and sometimes sleeping life of the great traditions of Christian experience, of which we are all the legacy and the future.

Therefore as a Catholic believer and theologian I want to talk about our Dutch Catholic church, which is nevertheless also worldwide, about its relationship with the world of men and women, its relationship with ecumenical Christianity and finally about its relationship to the rule of God over the world, the kingdom of God.

I. Outside the world of men and women there is no salvation

Belief in God as the ground and source of the existence of our world and the history of human freedom is not a belief on the same level as one's 'belief' in the existence of a faraway solar system in the universe. It is belief in God who wants liberation and salvation of and for people whom he brings to life. It is belief in the nearness of God to human beings in their history which makes them whole. No matter what circumstances we find ourselves in, through fortune or misfortune, through mere chance or our own fault, there is no place, no situation in which God is not near to us to save and in which we will not be able to find him. This does not mean that the circumstances in which we find ourselves are 'the will of God'. To talk about 'the will of God' is quite often blasphemy in a particular situation: it is the absolutizing of one's own vision projected on to God.

We cannot reduce the active saving presence of God to our Christian awareness or our experience of this presence. We cannot reduce salvation from God to the particular places of salvation that we call religions or churches. For the whole of our history rests and moves in God, who calls people to life and liberation. The world of human beings and its history are the basis of the whole reality of salvation; there salvation is achieved, liberation realized or... disaster brought on people. That means that our world of creation, our history in nature as our environment, is the sphere of God's saving action in and through human mediation. The history of religions, of churches, is only one segment of a broader human history. Religions are the place where particular people become explicitly aware of God's saving action in history. Moreover it is within this worldly history that religions have originated as movements in which there is experience (interpretative experience) of the salvation that God is actively realizing in the world. How else could religions come into being? Certainly not as something that could drop down from the sky. So it is a matter of recognizing that salvation is linked with the human world.

To sum up: salvation from God first of all comes about in the worldly reality of history and not primarily in the awareness of believers who know about it. The awareness of this is of course a separate gift, the significance of which we should not underestimate. But where good is furthered and evil challenged, where there is a plea for humankind in word and deed, by this historical praxis the nature of God – God as salvation for human beings, the foundation of universal hope – is indeed established, and moreover human beings also appropriate the gift of God's salvation: in and through the practice of love. The history of human beings and the life of human beings who hold on to one another or let one another go is the place where the cause of salvation or damnation is decided.

II. The churches: sacrament of salvation-in-the-world

So churches are not salvation; they are not the kingdom of God, but a 'sacrament' of the salvation and liberation which God wants to bring about through men and women in his world of creation. And if we do not put the church 'in its place', and at the same time 'in the place which is its due', if we forget this basic process of the salvation that must be brought about in the world, churches often become sectarian, clerical and apolitical. Churches are of the order of 'the sign': a sacrament of salvation. They are the explicit naming of salvation. Churches are called to be places where salvation from God is expressed, explicitly confessed, proclaimed prophetically and celebrated in the liturgy, with the aim of also in fact realizing salvation for men and women in everyday life. So there is a connection which must not be broken between 'world' and 'religion', world and church. The revelation and the concealment of God are identical in our belief in God. However, anyone who only has an eye to the concealment can in fact forget God, be silent about God and even ignore God. Religions and churches are then the recollection of the eternal will for salvation which is alive among us, of the absolute saving presence of God, the ground of human hope. Religions – synagogues and pagodas, mosques and churches – by their religious word, their sacraments or ritual and their praxis, prevent this universal presence of salvation from being forgotten.

But if the church is by definition related to the history of the world and what happens there, the churches understand themselves wrongly if they set themselves outside the strife of world history or if, on the other hand, they think that by their participatory and interpretative relationship to this world history they can neglect specifically religious forms: confession and word, sacrament and consistent praxis of faith in the world. The churches live from the salvation that God brings about *in the world*. Churches are a segment of our human history and are incomprehensible without this 'profane' history, just as this profane history becomes disastrous without the liberating action of inspired people.

Churches and religions are the grateful welcoming of the God who approaches in order to liberate and to call men and women to liberation. Confession and word, sacrament and praxis of faith, acting to heal people and open up communication, in the steps of Jesus, do not make confrontation with world history superfluous, whereas what really happens in events in the so-called 'outside world' makes talking in the language of faith necessary. It is precisely here that historical and also socio-political praxis in the world cannot be separated from the actions of proclamation, the sacraments and being the church. Anyone who breaks this connection damages the internal structure of religion and Christian action.

And yet the confessional language of church people and of their leaders is never a matter of speaking on their own authority but a gracious response to that which precedes all that believers say: God's creative action in history in and through men and women for the liberation and the salvation of men and women. It is men and women, believers within a particular tradition of experience, who 'give expression' to this action of God, make it Word. Only in this way can we speak of the Word of God, and then we do so rightly. God himself is the source of all our talk of God. We owe our confessional talk of God to the Creator who reveals himself to us. Therefore churches are also communities which speak *to* God, praying communities of faith and not simply one action group or another. Their praxis is to do what is spoken of in confession and liturgical prayer. Jesus, who in a unique way gave a visible human face to this universal saving will of the creator God in word and action, was sent to the cross by a secular, profane judgment. In this sense a historical, secular and political event is the central point of reference for the Christian churches – an event which these churches can then also rightly celebrate liturgically: at all events they are the 'sacrament' of the salvation that is brought about in the world.

III. The so-called 'classical' face of the church and the other face

1. In the Neoplatonic-hierarchical conception of the church the church forms a pyramid, a multi-stage system: God, Christ, the pope, the bishops, priests and deacons; below these the religious and then the 'laity': first the men and last of all the women and children. This post-Tridentine picture of the church held by the Jesuit Bellarmine and the Dominican Torquemada, afterwards accepted everywhere and further intensified since the nineteenth century, sees the church as a community organized around the pope of Rome, of whom the bishops are the prefects in every see, while the priests are the local representatives of these prefects, appointed to feed the sheep below them and far away. The ideological legitimation of this image of the church is based on two pillars: 1. the predominance of a christology which forgot the blowing of the Spirit over the lowermost parts of the church and in practice annexed the role of the Holy Spirit through the ministerial succession exclusively for the hierarchy; and 2. the social function of papal infallibility. In this view the Pope becomes the 'representative of Christ' in this world, just as the governors were the representatives of the Roman emperor in distant parts. So the gift of the Holy Spirit was reduced to an appropriation at a lower level, that of the believers, of what was said or decided at the top of the hierarchy. This picture of the church completely excluded the believers from the level on which decisions were made. The laity, above all the women, in it are no longer subjects, those who carry on and make church history: they become the objects of the priestly,

hierarchical and male care of souls. The ominous element in all this is above all the practical shift in the authority that particular papal acts could have in legally controlled, well defined circumstances, to the person of the pope himself, who was then said to be infallible as a person. It is then said that 'the pope is personally infallible' – which from a Roman Catholic perspective is a heresy, though it is one of the few heresies which has never been condemned from the official side.

Particular papal or conciliar decisions, taken in the name of the whole church community at the level of challenges which are vital for the gospel faith, can indeed be 'infallible', that is to say that in a more or less happy way they nevertheless give historical expression to Christian truth. This bears witness to the support of the Holy Spirit, which safeguards the unabbreviated gospel: but it does not elevate the person of the pope. The person of the pope here remains what he is: a personality who may be brilliant or mediocre, democratic or authoritarian. Even to move from this infallibility controlled by the law of the church to the person of the pope in fact robs all the other institutional authorities in the church, both the bishops and the community of faith, of their original Christian authority and authenticity. A personality cult of the pope as a consequence of this mysticism of infallibility overlooks the fact that the Peter function or the Petrine function of providing unity or communication involves only one office in the church, and thus is a ministerial service among many other ministries in the church.

2. The Second Vatican Council showed another face of the church. At least in theory, it broke away from the earlier picture of the church by defining the church (even before speaking of ministries in the church) as the people summoned by God among whom all believers are equal, believing subjects 'living from the Spirit': free children of God. Only after speaking of the people of God on the way to the final consummation does the Council speak of particular elements which give the church or the people of God organic structures. The differentiations in ministry which occur in this structuring do not affect the rights of the people of God as the subject of being-the-church. All ministries are there for that people, as a service. That these ministries are also particular charismas of the Spirit does not of itself say anything about institutional regulation and control in the church. Now the way in which the church organizes ministries makes impossible an institutional basis for the free play of the Holy Spirit among grass-roots believers. Moreover the fact that the ministry is a charisma of the Holy Spirit says nothing about the procedure for the appointment of ministers. In these matters the old church slogan was: 'what concerns all is also a matter for all'.

In its character as compromise, even Vatican II still points towards the pyramidal view of the church, albeit unintentionally. The Council defines from the start the right and duty of all believers also to be responsible for the church as *christifideles*, but from a later chapter (4) of *Lumen Gentium* it emerges that in practice a 'predetermined harmony' is postulated between the 'believed faith of the whole church community' and what the hierarchy proclaims and formulates as faith and policy, while believers get no claim in either the expression of the faith or in the government of the church.

To put it another way: on the basis of the will of Christ there can be no opposition between the content of faith in the life of a church community and what the pope or the hierarchy present. For – the argument goes – the object of the life of the people of God is the 'revealed mystery' and the object of proclamation; worship and government by the hierarchy is that same mystery, while the limits of the hierarchical authorities are the limits of revelation. So there is a smooth equilibrium, a positivistically postulated harmony, between the life of believers and the doctrine of the church hierarchy. This idyll of internal harmony has ominous consequences for the institution. For in that case any actual conflict between believers and hierarchy, and any conflict between a local church community and the top of the church, is assigned to the order of sinfulness. Moreover this view says nothing about the fact that church history has never been such an idyll. The actual history of conflicts is then *a priori* seen as the fruit of sin. Within this logic any conflict is resolved in favour of the stronger, i.e. hierarchical, position and declared by this side to be sin on the part of the other.

That there could also be conflicts which have nothing to do with sin but derive from differences, for example, even in matters of the gospel and pastoral work is in practice completely disregarded. This declaration that any conflict in the church is sinful puts the hierarchy in an immune or storm-free zone. People in fact continue to see the church as a *societas perfecta*, the perfected kingdom of God under the direction of Christ's representative. To the degree that the church is faithful, moreover, it has no real history: any actual conflicts that there ever were and still are are usually declared to be a history of human sinfulness. It is precisely because of this view, which is not just a view but church praxis, that many believers suffer over their church: at present there is much suffering over the faith in the church province of the Netherlands. Some people forget that if hierarchy and believers sometimes go divergent ways, these believers do this out of a gospel concern specifically for the church. And although we too are sinful men and women, within the ideological logic of this picture of the church in conflicts it is facile to divide believers bluntly into orthodox and freethinking. If the church hierarchy is fallible in most of its actions and nevertheless seeks in the power of the Spirit, through ups and downs, to keep the church commmunity on a gospel course, as I as a Christian believe, and if as a help in this, in some exceptional cases it can also prove 'infallible' – here of course showing an infallibility which, even according to the First Vatican Council, is merely the critical reflection of the firmness of the course of the whole of the church's community of faith – why should the right *a priori* lie with pope and bishops?

The co-responsibility of all believers for the church on the basis of our baptism in the Spirit essentially includes the participation of all believers in decisions relating to church government. How this participation is organized can vary in church history. Vatican II also gave at least some institutional prompting, to make this claim to participation possible: the Roman synods, the national councils, the conferences of bishops, the priestly councils, the diocesan and parish councils of lay believers and the frameworks of many Catholic organizations. But when these institutions bore fruit in practice – granted, sometimes in a good deal of variety – they were undermined from above and tamed. Moreover most administrative decrees after the Second Vatican Council predominantly play on one line of this council, so that the effectiveness of the other line in that same council does not get any institutional support and therefore – on the basis of the law of the tension between charism and institute – is doomed for the moment to disappear from the life of the church. One cannot in fact honestly speak of the equality of all in the church (Gal.3.26-28) if one does not specify or does not want to secure the institutional forms which follow from this equality.

IV. Church and ecumene

That the church is of the order of 'sacramentality' means that church and kingdom of God do not coincide. The kingdom of God is not 'of this world', but the church is really 'of this world': in this world it is 'openness to' the kingdom or rule of God over this world.

With the creed of the Council of Constantinople in 381 all Christian churches confess: 'I believe in one, holy, catholic and apostolic *ecclesia* or community of faith.' In the Second Vatican Council this was said of any local church in which the universal church is present as far as the local church lives in communion with the other local churches. But we know that this unity does not exist: the Christian churches are divided. We all suffer under our own sinfulness and that of our churches. So the four marks of the church do not describe our real churches in their historical forms, while on the other hand no church can produce a mystical distillation of the essence 'church': churches exist only in historical forms.

On the other hand this does not mean that these four marks of the church are purely eschatological, a reality of the final kingdom. It means that all Christian churches now already have elements which demand this unity, especially one God and one Lord, one baptism and one table. Because the four marks are fragmentarily present in all the churches, in mediocrity, in particular or 'parochial divisions', within all the churches they are nevertheless internal imperatives for change, calls really to follow the way to the final ecumenical consummation. The dynamism of the structural elements in all the churches does not call for this break: the gospel does not legitimate mediocrity; and the message proclaimed is not the basis for this enclosure in closed hiding-places. The four 'marks' of the church make a demand on all Christian churches for conversion. One cannot just call for the conversion of other Christian churches. All local and confessional churches are 'church' to the degree that they favour and encourage *communio*, communication with other local churches.

It is not scandalous that there are differences; it is scandalous that these differences are an obstacle to communion (people rightly do not want to make a comedy of unity, so they take the differences seriously). But a richly-patterned unity-in-communion does not call for a formal, institutional and administrative unity, far less a super-church. The four marks confessed are not a description even for the Roman Catholic church, but an imperative. Ecumene is not a private annexation of the gospel but a dispossession of the churches. There is plurality as a system of exclusion, but there is also plurality which does not call forth opposition but is experienced within the communion. Difference is only positive within communion with the other, who is different. There can be no authentic ecumene without an attempt to arrive at a theological understanding of the plurality of the churches: we must be able to believe the same thing – in different ways. There is no eternally valid model of unity; nor is there a prefabricated and compulsory model of unity. We need all the Christian churches for this ecumene; we are all striving for a coming unity, the model for which has not been provided by any individual church so far. Unity is future, not a return to an earlier state. Moreover there can be no community without conflicts... except in Utopia or in heaven! But this final consummation judges us today on the basis of our revolt against the inhumanity which still prevails in this present.

It was from such insights that the Jewish people arrived at the idea of calling a year of jubilee every seventh year, a year in which inhuman conditions that had developed in the meantime had to be repaired. For already at that time people knew the weakness of the human heart and the violence of structures which enslave people. You can also use the 'Thy will be done' of the Lord's Prayer to diminish people; a year of jubilee can only raise people up, dry their tears and bring them to mutual forgiveness, in justice and love. What we need is such a year of jubilee. The church is not the kingdom of God, so it may not be a political power. But the world is not the kingdom of God either, unless it is raised up and comforted in the life of those who are poor and humiliated, unemployed and oppressed, discriminated against and lonely every day. The church, our church, may not therefore escape into an apolitical and asocial inwardness.

This day, on the Malieveld at the Hague, 8 May 1985, may be something of a day of jubilee. It is not as if we were celebrating that we are right, but is so that we may (and with all of us here *can*) show another face of the church and say: judge whether we, as people of God in the footsteps of Jesus Christ, are contributing to making people whole and freeing them in the gospel. We too all know that a healed church in a healed world is not 'of this world'; but that the church and world contain an imperative to work here and now towards the making whole and healing of both the world and the church, a making whole of... people. In these attempts we may and can, as believers, see fragile but real prefigurings of the final consummation we have dreamed of, of the God who is concerned for human beings: in the gesture or the hand-wave of individuals, in the liberating action of our many dear fellow men and women as it opens up communication. We just live by God's liberating word and action: you and I, all of us, have a right to be there!

Note

1. The '8 May Movement' came into being on the occasion of the visit of Pope John-Paul II to the Netherlands. It is a mass movement of Catholics who are critical of the church. Since 1985 (on that occasion on '8 May'), they have met each year at the beginning of May for a great demonstration: attendance ranges between 10,000 and 13,000. The Roman Catholic episcopate in the Netherlands dissociates itself from the movement.

32

The other face of the church

The 8 May 1986 demonstration at 's Hertogenbosch

I. The political relevance of the gospel of the kingdom of God

The church is there for men and women and not vice versa. Only within this perspective can we continue to remain active within the church in a credible way, even if bishops refuse us the name 'Catholic'. I thought that we had been given this inalienable name on the basis of our baptism in the Spirit. We for our part do not refuse our pastors the name 'Catholic', though they should do their best not to be alienated from the flock. It is not for nothing that we are here in the cattle market halls of 's-Hertogenbosch. As Catholics, along with all those who are in solidarity with us, we have met together here: it is an intrinsic consequence of what happened at the Malieveld in The Hague last year. '8 May' is a dimension of our membership of the community of the church, the day on which we encourage one another with hope which as a result continues to be alive among us.

The church is not the mystery of God's presence in the world, for this saving presence precedes and goes beyond all churches. In the language of the reality of salvation the church comes in second place; it is the mystery of the *manifestation of* and the *message concerning* God's effective presence in the human world. Of that mystery all of us – here and outside – are a living element, a segment which does not declare itself to be immune from criticism or sociological analysis, but rather puts itself on show, as Paul says, 'We have become a spectacle to the world, to angels and to men.' 'We (here) are weak but you are strong. You (who do not want to come here) are held in honour, but we in disrepute' (I Cor.4.9b, 10-12); not found worthy still to be called 'Catholic', open to the interrogative gaze of all, outsiders and believers who show another face within the same church. Only, we know that on the basis of our baptism in the Spirit we have an identity which cannot be taken from us by any fellow human being or fellow believer.

In *De Brug*, a Nijmegen newspaper, the Protestant pastor J.Colijn, who has grateful memories of the 8 May meeting on the Malieveld last year, bewails the gulf between the Catholic religious enthusiasm of the 8 May movement and the absence from it of Roman Catholic bishops. As a Reformed Christian he notes that the bishops 'had little eye for the real background of what was alive here among many people... What a pity it was that there was no awareness that the question of renewal is rooted in a deep love for the church and its history. As a Protestant I experienced the great meeting in The Hague as a very liberating happening... I personally felt it to be a great lack that none of the bishops was present in The Hague'; 'a bishop could only be grateful for so much spiritual passion and so much longing for a clear church.' Thus Pastor Colijn. Who is leaving whom in the lurch?

Recently the deep insight that the church is a mystery has been much abused. Church communion as *mystery* cannot be found behind or above concrete visible reality. Church community is to be found *in* this reality which can be demonstrated here and now: we too, all of us assembled here, are a part of this living mystery, and we shall not allow anyone to take this religious reality from us. The 8 May movement is also a mystery as a phenomenon of the one great Catholica which is to be found in greater or lesser concentration in many believing Christian communities. In this assembly of men and women who have gathered here in the market halls at 's Hertogenbosch in the name of Jesus, confessed as the Christ, and in the name of many people who suffer in and over the church, today we celebrate the mystery of the church, of our being the church, with all who are present here a specific segment of the people of God, an honorific title which we shall let no one take from us. We shall not even let our Second Vatican Council be taken away from us under the mist of flowery lip service to that council.

Here, gathered together on Ascension Day, we do not stare in despair up to the clouds, to hear from the heavens above: 'People of Galilee, why do you stand looking into heaven? This Jesus who was taken up from you into heaven, will come in the same way as you saw him go into heaven' (Acts 1.11). And so, the Gospel of Luke says from its side, they went back to Jerusalem to their temple and their people (Luke 24.44-53). For God there is no dualistic distinction between 'here below' and 'there above': 'Thy will be done on earth, here among us as it has from of old been done in heaven', and 'Heavenly Father, forgive us our trespasses, as we too here on earth forgive one another our trespasses.' It is not that we can imitate heavenly relationships here on earth. It is rather that a kingdom of God will never come in fullness after our history unless we begin to build it here on earth, with both feet on the ground, hand in hand, shoulder to shoulder with our fellow men and women, pressing against one another, both in the opening up of interpersonal communication and in social and political commitment – two dimensions of one and the same love of neighbour which is the visible dimension of our love of God, and as a result a guarantee of the authenticity of our love of God. Although the coming kingdom of God is greater than anything that we can do here on earth, in any case we must make messianic preparations for our human world in the power of the Spirit which Jesus sends us, preparations for the gift of the kingdom of God, which otherwise will never be received. God still gives a future to what we can realize and will in fact have realized as an unfinished symphony. After a good deal of discussion the Second Vatican Council arrived at the following formulation: 'Far from diminishing our concern to develop this earth, the expectancy of a new earth should spur us on, for it is here that the body of a new human family grows, foreshadowing in some way the age which is to come. That is why, although we must be careful to distinguish earthly progress clearly from the increase of the kingdom of Christ, such progress is of vital concern to the kingdom of God, insofar as it can contribute to the better ordering of human society' (*Gaudium et Spes* III, 39; *Expensio modorum*, ch.3).

On various sides the 8 May movement is accused of making a theological reduction. We are said to be reducing or minimizing the faith of the church to social and political commitment and in so doing to be undermining the mystical dimension of the church. This charge lurked in the background of the special Synod of Bishops in Rome in 1985 and this polemic dominated the publicity among Dutch Christians as well because of a publication. Apart from the fact that there is nowhere any indication of who among us had in fact brought about this reduction, we must put a counter-question, the question whether or not another reduction is possible which seems to be just as dangerous, a reduction in which Christians speak only about the forgiveness of sins and eternal life, while in practice offering no opposition to the destruction of our natural environment, to the grinding down of human beings, women and men, in both society and the church; to the almost cynical blindness of many people to the real presence, among us, of the little ones and the least, and especially often unemployed people in our prosperous Western society. Dom Helder Camara once said: 'If I give the poor food they call me a saint. If I ask why they are poor, they call me a communist.' This charge is beginning to apply to us all.

But what is the content of eternal life, what is the meaning of love for the creator God, source of eternal life, for people who are making our earthly world a wilderness? What can be the communion of saints and in it the crucified but risen Lord as the bond of this communion of saints if here on earth we do not establish any communication among ourselves, do not have pity on our fellow human beings, are not open to fair criticism and do not try to turn our system into a better social and political order in which as far as possible everyone has a share in the good things of the earth? To what must and can God still give a transcendent future if we do not take care of the *historical* future of humankind, the subject of God's heavenly consummation? God gives a future not only to nothing, the nothing of the dry bones of Ezekiel's vision; he gives a divine future to the goodness and justice people really bring about and have brought about here on earth in a fragmentary but real way. The goodness and justice done by people for the benefit of others here on earth will also determine the form, the contextual colour of what we call the divine gift of eternal life. So the church must take seriously the criticism of its social and political commitment only if its arguments are not in fact up to the standards of political discourse or if its activity prevents the realization of social freedom, e.g. through mistaking basic political rights. So in the political position of the churches an appeal to God is legitimate only if it is a call to combat the absolutizing of politics and the world and thus to combat a demonizing of politics and the world. It is a commitment to the world along the lines of the twofold commandment about the unity of loving the neighbour and loving God (Matt.22.36-39).

On the other hand our earthly community will never be perfect: the kingdom of God is never fully realized within our history. This too is part of the nucleus of the gospel, which is nevertheless politically and socially relevant. Those who argue to the contrary will have to trample over dead bodies, will have to enslave human beings in their freedom in order to arrive at the justice they seek. There is in fact violence that finds its source in the fanatical utopia of a just world which can already be realized on earth here and now. This utopia in turn has claimed innumerable victims in our history. Making peace and doing justice as Jesus preached it warns us against that: for the sake of this message he lost his own life in a violent way. He preached a new kingdom that rightly was not based on an exchange of repressive and oppressive powers, but sealed the end of any enslaving power. However important it may be, even for Christians, politics does not have the last and definitive word. The most important problems do not have political solutions.

II. If politics does not cover the whole of reality...

That politics is not everything therefore means that a church committed politically on a human basis and for Christian motives is at the same time a mystical church. It is a praying and celebrating community of faith, but one which in its prayer and celebration also keeps alive the memory of the suffering of oppressed people. Jesus, too, belongs to the other side of our history and precisely for that reason his suffering is remembered in the eucharist, also to the shattering of all power which is built on injustice.

In fact we modern men and women can no longer think of God in terms of need and function, of interest, efficiency and utility for human beings. In this sense God transcends the category of the necessary, the useful and the contingent. 'There was no need of God!' People who do not believe in God also find their life in the world meaningful and exert themselves for a better, more human world. In this, neither believers nor non-believers have *per se* a greater wisdom or greater modesty. God is not to be reduced to a function of human beings, the world or society. God is there as pure gratuitousness, even pure freedom; every day new; without a reason. The important thing is therefore for us to make something visible for people of God's perfect gracious and forgiving, free saving nearness in each one of them. *Dieu a besoin des hommes* – God needs people – not in order to be God but in order to be a God for men and women.

If the fundamental symbol of God is the living human being – the image of God – then the place where human beings are humiliated, tortured and forgotten, as individuals or as a community, by persons or violent structures, is at the same time the privileged place where (above all in our time) religious experience, indeed mysticism, becomes possible – becomes possible precisely *in and through* a human action which seeks to give form to this symbol of God, the human being; seeks to raise people up and give them a voice. Only then do we come home to the liberating communion of our creator and thus the depths of ourselves. Then, freed from ourselves, freed also from alienating powers, we can live a liberating life for others: free to do good. Only then can we, as in powerful experiences of happiness, dwell in God mystically, though not yet remain there... at least not so long as there is still one person, woman or man, who is hungry, orphaned or wounded, sitting at the side or excluded. For as long as that is the case things are not well with us either. The 8 May movement is a movement of Christian hope, not a form of Christian triumphalism.

33

For the sake of the kingdom of God

On the celebration of the jubilee of a profession

Hardly had I grown out of my formative Dominican years than (at the age of barely thirty) I was appointed 'Magister studentium' in Louvain, i.e. spiritual director of young Dominicans during their three-year philosophical training and after that during their four-year theological training. For eleven years, I looked after in all about 140 young Dominicans, each of them for seven years, until the day when I was called to Nijmegen. After a short time I arrived at the insight that whatever religious life and the package of three vows classically associated with it might mean, my essential question to these young Dominicans must be: *are you personally happy with us?* You do not become a religious to lead a sad, unhappy and anxious life. Religious, I thought, must be happy and content, otherwise they had better go away. And for that, as I myself had experienced earlier, you must sometimes really struggle with yourself. For at that time I wanted to become a 'philosopher', but the Order said to me, 'Sorry, we now happen to need a theologian, not a philosopher.' I obeyed. Later I was called to Nijmegen; at that time I would have preferred to stay in Louvain. I obeyed, and went to Nijmegen. The consequence of these two acts of religious obedience – and I can now say this with pleasure – has become *the* happiness and *the* luxury of my life.

According to the Gospel of John there are many, many mansions in the Father's house. The oldest brother of the prodigal son therefore had at least some right to feel frustrated when on his return the runaway son was given a party and a calf was killed in his honour. The oldest brother had worked hard, year in year out, day in day out; he had done, in his father's presence, what was then expected of a beloved son. But he had never received thanks; his father had never killed a fatted calf nor even once let him have his fling! Sometimes we forget this contrariwise parable in the case of our own household. We give bouquets to outsiders, but seldom to one another, to members of our own house. In this way the human splendour fades from a community. Bouquets also come from outside to us. In fact we often mean more to outsiders, and they to us, than we do to other members of our house. In that case, I think, there is wear and tear to everything that has become an 'institution' (ourselves included). In my view the crisis of the religious life is not a crisis of this religious life itself but of the *institution* of monastic life. Therefore many people today are rightly looking for other forms of religious life, of community life or solitary life. But the fantasy of calling forth a new form of human and religious life which is worth living in our Dominican existence seems, at the moment at any rate, to be exhausted or... to be hindered.

There is no sense in talking in the abstract about *the* nature of religious life. Nor can we say that the three vows of poverty, obedience and chaste celibacy make up the *essence* of religious life.

If one can talk of 'the essence' of the religious life, this does not differ from Christian life as such, ours and yours. Certainly religious place the emphasis on their work for the kingdom of God, and indeed here they make an essential statement. And you could make that essential statement in many ways: by living alone or living in many degrees of partial or total community life. Moreover you could make it within the church's ministry or outside it. Leaving aside the principle of dispensation, Dominicans give essential form to it in community. So if I speak of religious life, I am doing so in concrete terms, in the form of community life, as a member in and of the Albertinum. And in that case *this* form of religious life is essentially living in a community, in which one makes a profession, i.e. binds oneself to a particular religious order or community. This communal life of like-minded people, equally concerned for the kingdom of God, of course has inevitable social and practical consequences.

However, it would be an overestimation of sexuality and poverty and at the same time an underestimation of human autonomy to think that through the surrender, first of human love, secondly of human possessions, and thirdly of one's autonomy, Christians can pay homage to God in the most eminent way, and that the heart of the religious life lies there. Let me make this quite clear: to live in a community which shares money and possessions in abstinence from explicit sexual activity under the leadership of superiors, or to live alone, or with just a few others, in celibacy with a pastoral intent, is a legitimate human way of life for anyone who can do it. But it is their, ours and my, personal, human choice, and the mode of living as such has nothing to do with the nature of God or with the nature of human beings and human sexuality. God can call Christians to particular dedication to the kingdom of God, inside or outside the ministry, inside or outside a community. That is the heart of the divine calling and thus also of our profession. But if you live together for religious and pastoral reasons, i.e. out of concern for the kingdom of God, this social life inevitably has practical consequences for the internal structure of that society, which then also, for example, needs a governing body, requires brotherly or sisterly sharing, and makes difficulties for the forming of families in one's own circle.

The three religious vows are one historically possible and, in the traditional form of communal life, even inevitable social and practical consequence of this form of life together. But as such they may not be nonchalantly derived from God, as if God himself had said that he is served most by abstinence and dissociation from marriage and autonomy. That would be a heresy in respect of our Christian belief in creation: being alone with God does not seem to be everything for people, just as God too did not find being alone all that much fun and therefore created heaven and earth and everything that is in them. 'God and God alone' as the ideal of human life is a piece of heretical human megalomania.

So on the one hand I would defend the right of Christians, if they so wish, to opt for celibacy (and hopefully they are then choosing what is good for themselves, even better or best for themselves). On the other hand I would dispute the view that living a celibate life without at least explicit sexuality *as such* has a *religious* significance. However, this view is still more alive than we think today among many people, including religious. In both cases we have believers who either marry but if as Christians then 'in the Lord', or who remain unmarried, but if as Christians, then equally 'in the Lord'. Only a living relationship to God in Jesus Christ gives a religious significance both to marriage (and to other interpersonal human relations) and to celibacy willingly adopted or forced on one by circumstances. I resolutely dispute that they have this religious significance in and of themselves. I therefore challenge both the twentieth-century religious mystification of marriage and the age-old Western Greek-Christian mystification of celibacy.

In themselves, both marriage and celibacy are religiously neutral, in the sense that both can be part of meaningful human existence even without belief in God, and, sometimes or often, are also experienced in a nonsensical frustrating way as a hell. These forms of life do not have any more value than other forms of human and Christian life and therefore cannot make up the nature of religious life any more than these others can. In and of themselves celibacy, poverty and obedience to fellow human beings do not have any religious dimension. They say more about the image of God and humankind held by those men and women who in their own view are right to make this choice than about God who is said to want it or to ask it of people and in so doing even give it priority. This last is downright untrue and moreover unbiblical.

If there is anything emphatically worth listening to from the revelation about radical life in accordance with the gospel, it is the demand, as disciples of Jesus, within the framework of special concern for the kingdom of God as a kingdom of liberated and free men and women, to show solidarity with all who are left in the lurch by society, their fellow human beings and the church.

We can only experience the so-called vertical dimension of our love of God in the horizontal dimension of human love and in the struggle for honesty, justice and peace – although God is always greater than our own heart and actions, and therefore a surplus of spirituality is always needed for us to be able to live in a truly religous way. Is not this what emerges when in the family bond of the Dominican family brothers and sisters gather in sisterhood and brotherhood – often despite themselves – with all those who work for peace, brought together in opposition to injustice? Is it not *this* which strengthens the bonds between us if here we remain uncrushable and full of trust? Has not the new thing already begun, even among us? Can you not see it?

Because Lucas Grollenberg and I, in all kinds of ups and downs, can look back happily and gratefully on what we have gained in the past from the Dominican order, but as we become older must leave to younger ones the future that is still to be made, like Moses and Aaron in their time, hoping to be able to see something of this near future, we want at all events to give thanks to God in this celebration of the eucharist.

VI · In Special Circumstances

34

I still have much to say to you

(John 16.12-15)

A homily at the celebration of the eucharist in a critical community[1]

Reading from the Gospel according to John:

'I have yet many things to say to you, but you cannot bear them now. When the Spirit of truth comes, he will guide you into all the truth, for he will not speak on his own authority, but whatever he hears he will speak, and he will declare to you the things that are to come. He will glorify me, for he will take what is mine and declare it to you. All that the Father has is mine; therefore I said that he will take what is mine and declare it to you' (John 16.12-15).

Homily

For the most part people live by stories which inspire them to action. Thus for example in Latin America many people live by the recollection of former incidents under their colonial occupiers. So the whole of the Old Testament lived by critical and dangerous recollections of past great deeds done in and through the people by the Lord. So the Christian community still lives today by the recollection of what God has done in and through Jesus, confessed as Messiah, for Israel as the messianic people, sacrament of the world.

In line with the biblical *anamnesis*, i.e. remembrance, the recollection of the story of God with and through human beings assembled round Jesus, the Christ, is not simply a recollection of what took place earlier. It is a narrative reference back to the past with a view to doing better in the present. So 'God recalls' his former acts of salvation by producing constantly new acts of liberation. So the belief of the Christian community is a recollection of the message and lifestyle of Jesus, a recollection of the life and death of the risen Jesus by a praxis of the community 'in the steps of Jesus'. It is a matter of a living tradition directed towards the future. Without tradition there is no community, not even a critical community. The living community is the only authentic relic that Jesus has left us; and the supreme living presence of it is the community, gathered together, celebrating the supper, the eucharist, 'in memory of him'.

Here we are right in the middle of the theme of the tradition about which the Gospel of John to which we have listened wanted to speak explicitly. Even the Holy Spirit will not bring anything new that has not already come about in Jesus in word and action. The Spirit will help us to clarify the riches of Jesus' gospel for coming generations, for us here and now, and to put it into practice in a way appropriate for today. In this sense 'tradition' is a fundamental keyword for any Christian community. Even a critical community cannot escape this. We all 'enter the story' in and through the story of the Christian or messianic community, that of former times and that of today, which hands on the story to our generation in words and in its living.

Without stories, without traditions, we would be deprived of *remembrance*; we would not find our own place *in the present* and would remain without hope or *expectation of the future*. The community would then stand outside all time and live in rarefied abstraction, perhaps as a kind of action group or as a praiseworthy mediation group, but not as a loyal and critical community of Jesus the Lord, a 'community of God'.

The critical question is therefore whether the life of this critical community is in fact a new chapter within the one great story of Israel, of Jesus and his messianic movement. For any community this question is a life-and-death question. It is a question which needs to accompany the life of any community. *Par excellence* this self-critical question belongs to the life of a community which explicitly calls itself critical – critical precisely as a community of Jesus, confessed as the Christ, the Son.

As the Critical Community of IJmond, all those years ago you began as a community which set itself apart critically from the complex whole in which, under all kinds of disguises and distortions, neverthless the great Catholic Christian tradition had come down to you. Much in it is felt to be oppressive, a hindrance to Christian identity. And this process of purging is far from being at an end. But in the meantime the situation has fundamentally changed, in the sense that the younger ones among you, who will increasingly take over the community as time goes on, are no longer opposed to what is called 'the tradition', for the simple reason that they do not even know the content of these traditions which their parents opposed. They never experienced the earlier situation, nor the pressures which the older ones among you experienced. But in this way they not only do not know what was oppressive in many traditions, but perhaps also do not know the precise content of this great tradition, the basic story of Israel and Jesus. This is a completely new situation on which we very much need to reflect. The *contextuality* in which a specific community stands must be the concrete agenda for the priorities which a community of Jesus has and perhaps must have.

I am beyond question also aware of the dangers which can be connected with this. I am not arguing in any way for nostalgia for the old, far less for a reactionary tendency which is rearing its head in many places, often against the deepest significance of Vatican II, and which is gradually and subtly getting the upper hand over a proclamation which argues for a revaluation of the great Christian tradition without which no community of God is possible and capable of sustaining life. What is at stake is the Christian identity of the messianic community, which is also critical of itself. The problem is not removed by careful avoidance of terms like 'Jewish-Christian tradition', 'church', 'God or Christ', to replace them by 'present challenges', 'community', 'mystery' and 'Jesus' – though it is sometimes a good thing to be more economical with words which are often misused by politics and power.

If we want to do justice to the word 'tradition' and above all to its reality, we must be careful to remember that this is a tradition of *experience*, in other words a handing down of what the Christian communities have experienced and done from and with Jesus, above all in and through their praxis of solidarity with a God concerned for humanity, moreover a God who wants a people of God concerned for humanity. Fundamentally that is tradition, and we cannot dispense with such a tradition without exhausting our resources.

In general human terms, quite apart from religious traditions, social and personal identity is inconceivable without tradition. No society, not even the most revolutionary one, starts from nothing; it finds inspiration in dangerous recollections. Therefore tradition really has a constructive significance: it can also teach us what we must change and what we must revive at any price as a value which has been acquired once and for all.

Therefore all cultural traditions express themselves in some basic stories which are told time and again; they also express themselves in rites the heart of which is laid down, and even in rarified formulae. If a society no longer believes in the tradition which supports it, not only does its tradition die but the society itself become aimless, without a direction and chaotic, and general disquiet arises. Not to know the tradition is not to know one's own society and ultimately not to know oneself. Any person, any society, any culture is as it were a crossroads where on the basis of the past the present takes an inventive attitude towards the future. The whole structure of the Old and New Testaments is built on this connection of past, present and future. No mortal is creative from nothing. To neglect or underestimate one of these three elements mutilates a person, his or her society and religion; it then leads either to pure traditionalism, which kills and throttles; to pure opportunism, arbitrary actualism which does not see the blind spots in its own time and its own eye; or pure futurism, a blind undirected concern for change.

We find this universal human cultural structure of our humanity and the power of tradition within it in all religions, and also in the Christian community. What does the community of faith do when it has a festal gathering? We then read from the foundation documents of the messianic, Christian movement, the Old and New Testaments. We get involved in age-old community rites of prayer and liturgy. We sing confessions which constantly go back to the heart of things. And finally we agree together what the community can do here and now, in conformity with the praxis of the kingdom of God. In this way, and only in this way, albeit sometimes in gripping new forms which are true to life, Christian identity is built up.

A living community does not live just by traditions, but must in turn create constantly new traditions, in which yet others can live their own lives. And as Christians we believe that there will always be enough people, men and women, to stand in this tradition and hand on the torch of the messianic movement.

The reading from the Gospel of John makes all this clear to us today. You cannot contrast tradition and the Spirit of God, which now drives us and makes us driven, or set them off against each other. By tradition, then, we do not mean any historical deposits, but what I John says: 'The message that we have heard from him and hand on to you.' 'That which was from the beginning, which we have heard, which we have seen with our eyes, which we have looked upon and touched with our hands, concerning the way of life – it is that of which we speak' (I John 1.5; 1.1). 'That which we have seen and heard we proclaim also to you, that you may have fellowship with us' (1.3). What we desperately need today is, to put it in theological terms, *a theory of the Spirit of God in terms of an ecclesiology*. Or more simply: a correct insight into the blowing of the Spirit of God in the form of what an authentic community is, says and confesses and actually does. And that applies both to church leaders and to the Christian community.

Precisely because of the danger that as a result of our actions, in place of a living tradition of faith, indwelt by the life-giving Spirit, tradition can also rigidify into well preserved mummies, interesting to have a nostalgic look at, but not appetizing to live from, we need basic communities within and alongside the great, perhaps somewhat cumbersome and 'traditional parishes', basic communities which are nevertheless in the form of a community of Jesus, the Christ. The theology of the local communities needs a theology of the universal church, as the bond of many communities in love. It needs this precisely so that your new experiences and your new praxis can be integrated into the great tradition of the church's experience, which will be enriched by it. At the same time this prevents these new experiences and this new praxis, in prayer and political commitment in keeping with the gospel, from just remaining sporadic, from failing to stimulate the church community as a whole, and ultimately from beginning to have a disintegrating effect, so that the critical community is driven in the direction of a ghetto or sect either through a lack of self-criticism or through a failure of the church hierarchy to understand. Permanent mutual brotherly and sisterly admonition is therefore an element in the health of the Christian identity.

Therefore I am standing here in your midst today, not so much as a theologian but as one who proclaims the word of God. New experiences must be confronted with all the assets of experiences and faith which have been accumulated in the centuries-long history of the Christian messianic movement. To close oneself off from them, not to allow oneself to be addressed by other Christian communities and their responsible leaders, is a shortcoming in Christian identity. So here there is both a call to ecumenism on the part of all the churches in our Dutch, European and world society, and especially a call to listen to what is happening in the churches of the Third World. And also in the church of Rome. This afternoon I noticed in your working groups how vividly this care is experienced in your community. But it must not be a one-way traffic, from here to the churches of the Third World. For not to want to listen to what other communities say, confess and do is arrogance towards the gospel. It would be to claim for oneself a monopoly in the understanding of the gospel and thus in the embodiment of the presence of the Holy Spirit. True universality, on the other hand, cannot be found in common denominators or pure uniformity, but lies in the radical confession of the genius of a Christian life which is shared in common, at the point where various living communities in different contexts communicate with one another. You yourselves have formulated this clearly in the slogan which I read this afternoon: 'Help us to remove the injustice in the world, beginning with IJmond, our own community.' And therefore beginning with our own hearts and actions.

Moreover no rules of thumb can be given for the task and duty of a critical community in the 1980s. On the basis of recollection of and participation in the great Christian tradition of experience, with an eye to the context in which you live, a critical community of Jesus Messiah will find sufficient inspiration and orientation in the genius of its own Christianity, inventive and listening, for transposing the praxis of the kingdom of God into the key of the historical situation of today.

And to the leaders of your critical community I say – not I, but the apostle Paul: 'We are not here to lord it over your faith, but we work with you for your joy' (II Cor.1.24). As 'labourers for the community' you 'proclaim the message of reconciliation' (II Cor.5.18), the message of liberation and of a God who is concerned for humankind and humanity. II Timothy 2.2 says this in its own way: 'What you have heard from me before many witnesses, entrust to faithful people (Paul says men) who will be able to teach others also.' This is the message of the gospel, told by me today, to your critical community.

Note

1. The 'Critical Community of IJmond' was originally a Catholic parish; because it has as its leaders married Catholic priests and also Protestant laity who have not been officially appointed, it operates outside the responsibility of the episcopate.

35

A right-wing schism

Bishop Marcel Lefebvre: dupe of a recent Roman Catholic church tradition

We must make a careful distinction between on the one hand the views of Lefebvre with his kindred spirits and on the other so-called followers who in fact have never been able really to accept the changes in the Catholic liturgy. No one grudges them a Latin mass, even 'with three priests', provided that they do not grudge others their new liturgy. But the authentic Lefebvrists are concerned with something quite different. They are people, above all French people, who still live in the spirit of Maurras and Action Française: people who do not accept the legitimate achievements of the French Revolution: freedom of conscience, freedom of religion, pluralism, tolerance and 'ecumenism', democracy and so on. It is characteristic of the movement that Lefebvre advised his supporters to vote for the ultra-right-wing J.-M.Le Pen as President of France. Lefebvre has said publicly that his political models are: from the past, Pétain, Franco and Salazar; and today, the dictator Pinochet and Le Pen. Lefebvre is one of four who voted no to many things in the solemnn final session of Vatican II.

However, we should not forget that in the nineteenth century and the beginning of the twentieth a number of solemn papal encyclicals (*Syllabus, Quanta Cura*, etc.) had defended precisely what Lefebvre is now asserting, and declared heretical what Lefebvre now regards as heresy. Therefore from a church-political and theological perspective I find it quite perverse that the principle of authority is used exclusively against Bishop Lefebvre. He himself can appeal to papal authority just as well, especially that of Pius IX (who condemned both liberalism and socialism), Pius X (who rejected all 'modernistic' tendencies), Pius XI and Pius XII, although the Lefebvrists then forget that Pius XI in 1926 also condemned Action Française. However, church tradition is a living and developing reality. To make a reference to, for example, only one pope without seeing what he says and interpreting it in the light of all scripture and the whole living tradition of the church becomes sheer dogmatism and fundamentalism. So on both sides the exclusive reference to 'church authority' seems to me to be an unsound undertaking. Authority is then set over against authority in the discussion, while people miss what it is realy about.

Meanwhile this schism of people who truly think like Lefebvre is not very important. It involves a handful of believers who live almost exclusively in the France of Le Pen, in the French-speaking Swiss canton of Le Valais where Eĉone is situated, and in some south German dioceses. It is a movement which already existed in more or less latent form before the Second Vatican Council. Some years after the Council, in November 1970, Lefebvre (initially even with the permission of his bishop, Mgr Charrière), established the 'brotherhood of St Pius X'. This was a community life but without vows, as a brotherhood under diocesan law. Priests, brothers and female religious could be members. The brotherhood now numbers 260 active priests, spread over twenty-eight countries, and 300 seminarians. (By comparison the official seminaries of the French episcopate counted 1,196 seminarians in the academic year 1986-1987.) The French branch is the strongest. It is reckoned as being about 5000 core members, fifteen priories, three abbeys and five carmels under the direction of Mère Marie Christiane, Mgr Lefebvre's sister. The 'Quartier General' of the French is in the church of Saint Nicolas du Chardonnet in Paris. In addition to gifts from supporters, money comes above all from extreme right-wing circles, although this is not mentioned too loudly. Although there is no institutional connection between the brotherhood and the French National Front, there are many personal associations.

The Vatican is now confronted with the problem of the reception of many supporters who do not want to follow Lefebvre into his schism, and that is practically all the believers who followed him only because of their nostalgia for the old Latin mass, of which Lefebvre is the catalyst. But this schism of 'right-wing conservatives', while people were wrongly always afraid of a left-wing or at least progressive schism, will have consequences for whatever is called an 'open church' or 'critical church'. The concessions which the Vatican made to Lefebvre at the beginning of May 1988 point in the direction of a much stricter interpretation of the Second Vatican Council. The schism will give an advantage to Opus Dei and make the situation of the so-called progressive believers in the church even more difficult. In this sense this schism, which is extremely small in extent and will be even smaller in the future (for example, only a few hundred Lefebvrists are known in the Netherlands), is far more dubious for the health of the whole of church life than some people suppose. It is also a known fact that some Curia cardinals are, if not followers, at least kindred spirits of Lefebvre, and were themselves ready for concessions which flout the Second Vatican Council.

In my view the schism of Bishop Lefebvre is less a directly religious schism than a *de facto* religious schism with a major social and political background. The schism will continue as long as the spirit of Action Française remains alive. But also the spirit of any integralism. Ultimately it is striking that this break is really a schism of an integralist clergy which thinks that it can dictate the terms of the truth: of some conservative priests and religious. The believers who in nostalgia only long for a Latin and Gregorian mass are its dupes.

36

Closing prayer

A psalm prayer

Are you only a God who is near at hand;
not also a God who is far away (Jer.23.23)?

You are a hidden God (Isa.45.15).

Or do you hide your face from us,
to see what our end will be (Deut.32.20)?
And yet:
You do not afflict and humiliate (Lam.3.33).

You are ready to be sought
by those who do not ask after you;
you are ready to be found
by those who do not seek you (Isa.65.1).

Do I seek you in chaos (Isa.45.19c)?

I hear, 'I the Lord, announce your salvation
and proclaim what is just.'
But poor and needy seek water,
and there is none,
their tongue is parched with thirst (Isa.41.17).
How can my soul be still
over you, God, who are my salvation? (Isa.64.4)

May you find those who do right (Isa.64.6)!

Then we can all say,
you are our God, a liberator of humankind.

You have heard my cries;
you have heard me and said:
'Be not afraid' (Lam.3.51).
'Behold, I am doing a new thing;

now it springs forth,
do you not perceive it?' (Isa.43.19).

Lord, I believe,
help my unbelief (Mark 9.24b).

And teach me, poor fool,
how I must pray (Guido Gezelle).

OCCASIONS AND PUBLICATIONS

1. Homily on the Twenty-second Sunday of the Year (Year C). Readings: Numbers 15.32-36 and Luke 14.1-7. Albertinunm, Nijmegen, 31 August 1986.

2. Homily on the Fourteenth Sunday of the Year, 6 July 1986. Readings: Isa.66.10-14c; Luke 10.1-9. Nijmegen, 26 July 1986.

3. Homily on the Twenty-third Sunday of the Year. Readings: Isaiah 35.4-7a; Mark 7.31-37. Nijmegen, 4 September 1988.

4. Homily on the Twenty-Seventh Sunday of the Year. Readings: Habakkuk 1.2-3, 2.2-4; Luke 17.5-10. Albertinum, Nijmegen, 5 October 1986.

5. Homily on the Twenty-fourth Sunday of the Year (Year A). Reading: Matthew 18.21-35. Nijmegen, 13 September 1987.

6. On the occasion of a solemn profession at which the religious had chosen John 3.1-13 as a reading. Rotterdam, 4 November 1984.

7. Homily. Readings: II Sam.12.7-10; Gal.2.16, 19-21; Luke 7.36-50. Nijmegen, 12 June 1983. Published in *Reliëf* 52, 1984, no.3, 84-7.

8. Homily on the Fifth Sunday in Lent. Readings: Jeremiah 31.31-34; John 12.20-32. Nijmegen, 20 March 1988.

9. Homily on the First Sunday in Advent. Albertinum, Nijmegen, 27 November 1983.

10. Homily on the Third Sunday in Lent. Readings: Exodus 20.1-17; John 2.13-25 (Year B), Nijmegen, 10 March 1985.

11. Homily on the Fifth Sunday after Easter. Reading: John 14.1-12. Nijmegen, 20 May 1984.

12. Christmas meditation, published in *De Bazuin*, Christmas 1983.

13. Homily on the reading Matthew 3.12-17 (Year A). Nijmegen, 11 January 1987.

14. Homily on the First Sunday in Lent (Year A). Albertinum, Nijmegen, 8 March 1987.

15. Epiphany (Year B). Nijmegen, 3 January 1988.

16. Palm Sunday. Albertinum, Nijmegen, 23 March 1986.

17. Good Friday meditation. Albertinum, Nijmegen, 28 March 1986.

18. Pentecost. Albertinum, Nijmegen, 22 May 1988.

19 Sacrament Day. Albertinum, Nijmegen 1987. Already published in *Kerygma* 31, 1987/1988, no.4, pp.34-8.

20. Christ the King. Readings: Ezekiel 34.11-17; Psalm 23; Matthew 25.31-46. Albertinum, Nijmegen, 25 November 1984.

21. Lenten meditation: 'You are a hidden God' (Isa.45.15). Nijmegen, 14 March 1986. Already published in *Tijdschrift voor Geestelijk Leven* 43, 1987, 27-30.

22. Already published as 'Gods "weerloze overmacht"', *Tijdschrift voor Theologie* 27, 1987, 370-81.

23. Already published as 'Straffende gerechtigheid of liefde?', *Tijdschrift voor Geestelijk Leven* 44, 1988, 179-93.

24. Already published in *Optiek. Dominicaanse Familie* 11, 1986, no.3, 12-13.

25. At the high feast of St Dominic. Albertinum, Nijmegen, 4 August 1985.

26. KRO broadcast, 1987; an abbreviated form appeared in *Bewogen grensgangers*, Hilversum 1987, 57-60.

27. At the commemoration of John XXIII by the Catholic University of Nijmegen, published in *De Bazuin* 71, 1988, no. 17, 2-5; 18, 3-7.

28. Published in *Uit de grond van ons hart. Open brieven aan paus Johannes Paulus II* (ed. Michel van der Plas), Weesp no date, 293-8.

29. Published in *De Bazuin* 71, 1988, no. 1, 3-5.

30. Published as 'Boodschap en praxis van het rijk Gods', *Wending* 43, 1988, no.4, 204-6.

31. At the first demonstration of the 8 May Movement, published in *De Bazuin*, special 8 May number 68, 1985, 14-18.

32. At the second demonstration of the 8 May movement on 9 May 1986. Published in *De Bazuin*, special number 69, 1986.

33. At the jubilee of the profession of L.Grollenberg and E.Schillebeeckx; homily at the celebration of the eucharist. Albertinum, Nijmegen, 21 September 1986. Published in *De Bazuin* 68, 1985, 1-2.

34. Sermon during a service of the 'Critical Community of IJmond', 5 September 1981.

35. Published in *Volkskrant*, 13 July 1988.

36. A version of this prayer also appeared in *God is New Each Moment*, T.&.T.Clark 1983, 127f.